# OUTLOOK 2000® QUICK REFERENCE

*Sherry Kinkoph*

Que Corporation, 201 West 103rd Street, Indianapolis, Indiana 46290

## MICROSOFT® OUTLOOK 2000® QUICK REFERENCE

**Copyright © July, 1999 by Que Corporation**

All rights reserved. No part of this book shall be reproduced, stored in a retrieval system, or transmitted by any means, electronic, mechanical, photocopying, recording, or otherwise, without written permission from the publisher. No patent liability is assumed with respect to the use of the information contained herein. Although every precaution has been taken in the preparation of this book, the publisher and author assume no responsibility for errors or omissions. Neither is any liability assumed for damages resulting from the use of the information contained herein.

International Standard Book Number: 0-7897-2113-9

Library of Congress Catalog Card Number: 99-62553

*Printed in the United States of America*

First Printing: July, 1999

01    00    99                    4    3    2    1

## TRADEMARKS

All terms mentioned in this book that are known to be trademarks or service marks have been appropriately capitalized. Que cannot attest to the accuracy of this information. Use of a term in this book should not be regarded as affecting the validity of any trademark or service mark. Microsoft Outlook is a registered trademark of Microsoft Corporation.

## WARNING AND DISCLAIMER

Every effort has been made to make this book as complete and as accurate as possible, but no warranty or fitness is implied. The information provided is on an "as is" basis. The authors and the publisher shall have neither liability nor responsibility to any person or entity with respect to any loss or damages arising from the information contained in this book.

| | | |
|---|---|---|
| **Executive Editor**<br>Greg Wiegand | **Copy Editor**<br>Fran Blauw | **Cover Designers**<br>Dan Armstrong<br>Ruth Lewis |
| **Acquisitions Editor**<br>Stephanie McComb | **Indexer**<br>Mary Gammons | **Copy Writer**<br>Eric Borgert |
| **Development Editor**<br>Nick Goetz | **Proofreader**<br>Maribeth Echard | **Layout Technician**<br>Mark Walchle |
| **Managing Editor**<br>Tom Hayes | **Technical Editor**<br>Ben Schorr | |
| **Project Editor**<br>Karen S. Shields | **Interior Designer**<br>Louisa Klucznik | |

# ABOUT THE AUTHOR

**Sherry Kinkoph** has authored more than 30 computer books for Macmillan Computer Publishing over the past six years. Her recent publications include *How to Use Microsoft Office 2000*, *The Complete Idiot's Guide to Excel 2000*, and *Sams Teach Yourself Quicken 99 in 10 Minutes*.

Sherry began exploring computers in college, and claims that many a term paper was whipped out using a trusty 128KB Macintosh. Today, Sherry's still churning out words, but now they're in the form of books, and instead of using a Mac, she's moved on to a trusty PC. A native of the Midwest, Sherry currently resides in Fishers, Indiana, and continues her quest to help users of all levels master the ever-changing computer technologies.

# DEDICATION

To my nephews, Jacob and Joshua Cannon—may you
always have a great *outlook* on life.

# ACKNOWLEDGMENTS

Special thanks to Stephanie McComb for her excellent acquisitions work; to Nick Goetz for putting his development expertise to such good use; to Fran Blauw for dotting the i's and crossing the t's; to Karen Shields for shepherding this book every step of the way and making sure it made it to the printer on time; and to Ben Schorr for checking the technical stuff and ensuring that all the steps work as promised. Finally, extra special thanks to the production team for assembling this handy reference and making it all look so nice.

# INTRODUCTION

Outlook 2000 is the latest version of Microsoft's popular personal information management program. It's the perfect tool for organizing your schedule, sending and sorting email, tracking tasks, and keeping a record of names and addresses, along with a myriad of other features. So how do you go about learning all the nifty things the program can do? You can certainly pick up a book on the subject; there are dozens to choose from and each offers you detailed information about how the program works. But what if you don't have time to wade through an information-packed book to find what you're looking for? What if you just want to know the specifics for performing a certain task? What if you just want the nitty-gritty, no-frills facts for using Outlook? If that's the case, welcome to *Microsoft Outlook 2000 Quick Reference*, a reference book designed specifically for people on the go.

*Microsoft Outlook 2000 Quick Reference* presents you with the pertinent information you need to complete a task without explaining why it works that way or demonstrating the gazillion other options doing the same thing. Instead, you get just the steps you need to quickly use a feature. The compact size and spiral binding make it easy to flip to the information you need fast, and keep it available while you try out the steps yourself.

## HOW TO USE THIS BOOK

Each Outlook 2000 topic is arranged alphabetically in the book. Use the table of contents or the index to look up the feature or action you want to perform.

For example, if you want to find out how to send an email message, look under the topic **Email** in the **E** section of the book. Depending on the topic, you might find a variety of related subtopics. Email, for instance, includes subtopics on sending a message, replying to a message, and sending a blind carbon copy of a message.

Each subtopic lists the specific steps to complete the task. That's it. No lengthy text to read, no explanations; just the bare-bones information you need to use the feature.

This book covers all the main Outlook features and major tasks you might want to perform. The back of the book includes an introduction to Outlook for new users.

## CONVENTIONS USED

The steps found under each topic are short and to the point. When you need to select a menu command, the command appears in bold type, such as "choose **Tools, Accounts**." (This means open the **Tools** menu and choose the **Accounts** command.) Any icon buttons you need to click are shown as they appear onscreen, such as "click the **Print**  button."

Keyboard shortcuts are written like this:

Press Ctrl+X.

(This means you must press the Ctrl key and the letter X at the same time.) These shortcuts also appear in **bold type**.

In addition, you'll find Quick Tips tables that show you the quickest way to perform a task:

*Quick Tips*

| *Feature* | *Button* | *Keyboard Shortcut* |
|---|---|---|
| Create a new appointment | New | Ctrl+Shift+A |

Plus, you'll find tip boxes scattered throughout that offer additional information about the topic when applicable.

## ACCOUNTS

Outlook 2000 taps into your Internet account or network server to let you send and receive email and view Web pages. When you installed Outlook, you had a choice of using Internet Only or Corporate or Workgroup mode. Use Internet Only mode if you use a modem to connect to your Internet account. Use Corporate/Workgroup mode if you connect through a network server.

### View the Internet Accounts List in Internet Only Mode

1. Choose **Tools, Accounts**. This opens the Internet Accounts dialog box.
2. Select the **Mail** tab, if it's not already displayed, to view a list of email accounts.
3. Click the [ Close ] button to exit the dialog box.

> **TIP**
>
> The **Accounts** command (found on the **Tools** menu) is available only if you're using Outlook in Internet Only mode. Another way to find out whether you're using Internet Only or Corporate/Workgroup mode is to choose **Help, About Microsoft Outlook**.

### Set Up a New Mail Account for Internet Only Mode

1. Choose **Tools, Accounts**.
2. Select the **Mail** tab.
3. Click the [ Add ▶ ] button and choose **Mail** from the list.
4. The Internet Connection Wizard opens. Follow the directions on each screen to set up the account, clicking the [ Next > ] button to continue each time.
5. At the last wizard screen, click the [ Finish ] button. Your new account is added to Outlook's list of Internet accounts.
6. Click the [ Close ] button to exit the Internet Accounts dialog box.

> **TIP**
> Click the `< Back` button to return to a previous wizard screen, or click the `Cancel` button to cancel the wizard entirely. If you need help with a wizard screen, click the `Help` button.

### Change Account Properties for Internet Only Mode

1. Choose **Tools, Accounts**. Then select the **Mail** tab.
2. Double-click the account you want to change.
3. Use the **General** tab to make changes to the account name and your email address.
4. Use the **Servers** tab to change your incoming mail (POP3) and outgoing mail (SMTP) information.
5. Use the **Connection** tab if you need to change your type of connection (such as local area network or a phone line) or the modem you use to connect.
6. Click the `OK` button to close the Properties dialog box and apply any changes.
7. Click the `Close` button to exit the Internet Accounts dialog box.

> **TIP**
> To change from Internet Only mode to Corporate/Workgroup mode, open the **Tools** menu and select **Options**, click the **Mail Delivery** tab, and then click the **Reconfigure Mail Support** button. This opens the Outlook 2000 Startup Wizard, and you can change your email configuration.

### Remove an Account in Internet Only Mode

1. Choose **Tools, Accounts**, and select the **Mail** tab.
2. Select the account you want to remove.
3. Click the `Remove` button.
4. Click the `Yes` button to remove the account.
5. Click the `Close` button to exit the Internet Accounts dialog box.

### Change the Default Mail Account for Internet Only Mode

1. Choose **Tools, Accounts**, and select the **Mail** tab.
2. Select the account you want to make the default account.
3. Click the `Set as Default` button.
4. Click the `Close` button to exit the Internet Accounts dialog box.

### View the Services List in Corporate/Workgroup Mode

1. Choose **Tools, Services**. This opens the Services dialog box.
2. Select the **Services** tab, if it's not already displayed, to view a list of services.
3. Click the `OK` button to exit the dialog box.

> **TIP**
>
> The **Services** command (found on the **Tools** menu) is available only if you're using Corporate/Workgroup mode.

### Set Up a New Account for Corporate/Workgroup Mode

1. Choose **Tools, Services** and select the **Services** tab.
2. Click the `Add...` button.
3. Select the service you want to add and click `OK`.
4. Fill out the Properties dialog box fields with the information required for the type of service you selected.
5. Click `OK` to exit the Properties dialog box.
6. In the prompt box that appears, click `OK`. The service will be available the next time you start Outlook.
7. Click `OK` again to exit the Services dialog box.

### Change Account Properties for Corporate/Workgroup Mode

1. Choose **Tools, Services** and select the **Services** tab.
2. Select the service you want to change.

3. Click the `Properties` button to open the Properties dialog box associated with the service you selected.
4. Make any changes to the Properties dialog box fields.
5. Click `OK` to exit the Properties dialog box.
6. Click `OK` again to exit the Services dialog box.

> **TIP**
>
> To change from Corporate/Workgroup mode to Internet Only mode, open the **Tools** menu and select **Options**, click the **Mail Services** tab, and then click the **Reconfigure Mail Support** button. This opens the Outlook 2000 Startup Wizard, and you can change your email configuration.

**Remove an Account in Corporate/Workgroup Mode**

1. Choose **Tools, Services**, and select the **Services** tab.
2. Select the service you want to remove.
3. Click the `Remove` button.
4. Click the `Yes` button to remove the service.
5. Click the `OK` button to exit the Services dialog box.

## ADDRESS BOOK

Outlook's Address Book feature organizes email addresses for people you send email to. Instead of typing a new email address each time you want to send a message, select the address stored in the Address Book. You can organize your email addresses into groups and send a single message to everyone on the group list. If you have an existing address book in another program, you can import it into Outlook to use.

| Quick Tips |  |  |
|---|---|---|
| Feature | Button | Keyboard Shortcut |
| Address Book |  | Ctrl+Shift+B |

**Add an Address**

1. Click the **Address Book**  button on the Outlook toolbar to open the Address Book.

Address Book toolbar

List of email addresses

2. Click the New button on the Address Book toolbar and choose **New Contact** from the drop-down list.

3. On the **Name** tab, start entering information about the person. Click inside each field's text box and enter the appropriate information, as needed.

4. To add an email address, click inside the **E-Mail Addresses** text box and enter the email address. Then click the **Add** button to add the address to the list box.

5. Use the other tabs to enter additional details about the person, such as mailing address and business phone number. (The information you enter also will appear on the address card for this person in Outlook's Contacts folder.)

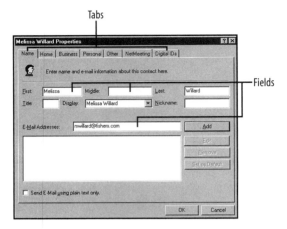

Tabs — Fields

6. When finished, click the **OK** button.

7. Click the **Close** ✗ button in the upper-right corner of the Address Book to close the Address Book.

> **TIP**
>
> More than one email address for the same person? Make one the default address. Select the address in the Properties dialog box, and then click the **Set as Default** button.

### Edit an Address

1. Click the **Address Book** button on the Outlook toolbar to open the Address Book.
2. Double-click the name you want to edit in the Address Book.
3. Use the various tabs in the Properties dialog box to make changes to the information for that person.
4. When finished, click the **OK** button.
5. Click **Close** ✗ to close the Address Book.

### Delete an Address

1. Click the **Address Book** button on the Outlook toolbar to open the Address Book.

2. Select the name you want to remove in the Address Book.
3. Click the **Delete** ⊠ button.
4. Click the `Yes` button to confirm the deletion.
5. Click **Close** ⊠ to close the Address Book.

### Create a New Group and Add Names

1. Click the **Address Book** 📖 button on the Outlook toolbar to open the Address Book.
2. Click the New 📖▾ button on the Address Book toolbar and choose **New Group** from the drop-down list.
3. Enter a name for the group list in the **Group Name** text box.
4. To add people from your existing list of names, click the `Select Members` button.
5. From the Select Group Members dialog box, select a name you want to add to the group. Then click the `Select ->` button.
6. Continue adding to the Members list, and then click the `OK` button to return to the Group Properties dialog box.
7. Click the `OK` button again to return to the Address Book.
8. Click **Close** ⊠ to close the Address Book.

> **TIP**
> To add a new name to the Members list, click the `New Contact` button and enter the person's name and email address. Click `OK` to return to the Select Group Members dialog box. You can now select the name from the list and add it to the group.

### Find an Address

1. Click the **Address Book** 📖 button on the Outlook toolbar to open the Address Book.

2. Click the **Find People** button on the Address Book toolbar.
3. Use the fields in the Find People dialog box to help you search for the address. Enter the name of the person you're looking for in the **Name** text box, for example.
4. If you know additional information that would help you locate the address, enter it in the remaining text boxes.
5. Click the [Find Now] button.
6. The bottom of the dialog box lists the results of the search. To view the address information, double-click the found address.
7. Click the [Close] button to close the Find People dialog box.
8. Click the **Close** button to close the Address Book.

> **TIP**
> To locate the email address of someone on the Web, click the **Look In** drop-down arrow in the Find People dialog box and choose a directory service. Outlook logs you onto the Web, where you can search for the person.

**Import an Address Book**

1. From the Outlook window, choose **File, Import and Export**.
2. The first Import and Export Wizard dialog box appears. Select **Import Internet Mail and Addresses** and click the [Next >] button to continue.
3. Select the type of program you're importing from, such as Outlook Express or Netscape Mail.
4. Enable the **Import Address Book** check box if it's not already enabled. Then click the [Next >] button to continue.
5. Choose where you want to import the addresses (in most cases, the Outlook Contacts folder will be fine), and then choose an option for handling duplicate addresses.

**6.** Click the `Finish` button to complete the import.

### Export an Address Book

**1.** From the Outlook window, choose **File, Import and Export**.

**2.** In the first Import and Export Wizard dialog box that appears, select **Export to a File** and click the `Next >` button to continue.

**3.** Select the type of export file you want to create, such as an **Access Database** or a **Comma Separated Values** file type; click the `Next >` button to continue.

**4.** Select the **Contacts** folder from which to export your address information and click the `Next >` button.

**5.** Choose where you want to export the data. Use the `Browse ...` button to locate a folder, and then click the `OK` button. Click the `Next >` button to continue to the next Wizard step.

**6.** Click the `Finish` button to complete the export.

*See Also* Contacts, Email, Personal Distribution List

# APPOINTMENTS

| Quick Tips | |
|---|---|
| *Feature* | *Keyboard Shortcut* |
| Create a new appointment | Ctrl+Shift+A |

Outlook's Calendar feature can help you maintain your daily schedule by setting appointments and meetings. If you're using Outlook in a network environment, you can schedule meetings with other users. You can assign a reminder alarm to an appointment that visibly and audibly reminds you of an upcoming engagement with a prompt box that pops up on your screen. Use the Appointment form to add or edit details about the appointment.

### Set an Appointment with the Appointment Form

1. From any Outlook folder, click the ![New] button's drop-down arrow on the Outlook toolbar and choose **Appointment** from the list, or press **Ctrl+Shift+A** on the keyboard.

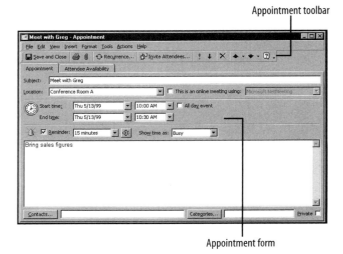

Appointment toolbar

Appointment form

2. Click inside the **Subject** text box and enter a subject title for the appointment, such as a person's name or type of appointment.

3. If applicable, click inside the **Location** text box and type a location.

4. Click the first **Start Time** drop-down arrow and choose a date for the appointment. Then click the second **Start Time** drop-down arrow and choose a time.

5. Use the **End Time** fields to specify when the appointment ends.

6. Optional: Use the **Notes** text box to add any notes about the appointment.

7. When you are finished filling out the Appointment form, click the ![Save and Close] button on the Appointment toolbar.

**11**

### Set an Appointment from the Calendar Folder

1. Click **Calendar** 📅 on the Outlook Bar to open the Calendar folder.

2. Double-click on the time slot for the date you want the appointment to occur.

3. Fill in the Appointment form fields as needed.

4. When you are finished filling in the details, click the 💾 Save and Close button on the Appointment toolbar.

### Set a Recurring Appointment

1. Press **Ctrl+Shift+A** on the keyboard to open the Appointment form.

2. Click the 🔄 Recurrence... button on the Appointment form toolbar.

3. Click the **Start** drop-down arrow to select a start time.

4. Click the **End** drop-down arrow and choose an end time, or use the **Duration** drop-down arrow to change the length of the appointment.

5. Choose a Recurrence pattern: **Daily, Weekly, Monthly,** or **Yearly**.

6. Depending on the pattern you chose, select from the options on the right side of the dialog box to indicate exactly how you want the pattern to recur.

7. Use the **Range of Recurrence** options at the bottom of the dialog box to specify how long the recurrence goes on.

8. Click the OK button to return to the Appointment form where you can enter more details about the appointment.

9. When you are finished filling in the details, click the 💾 Save and Close button on the Appointment toolbar to save and exit the Appointment form.

---

**TIP**

To set a new recurring appointment from the Calendar folder, choose **Actions, New Recurring Appointment**.

## Assign a Reminder

1. Press **Ctrl+Shift+A** on the keyboard to open the Appointment form and fill in the appointment details, as needed.

2. To assign a reminder to the appointment, click to place a check in the **Reminder** check box (if there isn't one already).

3. Click the **Reminder** drop-down arrow to specify the length of time prior to the appointment that you want to be reminded, such as 15 minutes, or type a reminder time directly into the text box.

4. When you are finished filling in the Appointment form, click the [Save and Close] button on the Appointment toolbar to save and exit.

---

**TIP**

Leave Outlook open to hear the reminder alarm. Click the **Minimize** [_] button in the upper-right corner of the Outlook window to minimize the program so you can work on other programs but still hear any reminder alarms.

---

## Set an Appointment's *Show Time As* Setting

1. Press **Ctrl+Shift+A** on the keyboard to open the Appointment form and fill out the appropriate fields, as needed.

2. To change how others view the appointment time on the network as well as color code how you view the appointment in your own schedule, click the **Show Time As** drop-down arrow and choose **Free**, **Tentative**, **Busy**, or **Out of Office**.

3. Optional: To mark the appointment as private so that others on the network won't see details about the appointment, enable the **Private** check box in the bottom-right corner of the form.

4. Click the [Save and Close] button to save the appointment.

## Assign a Category

1. Press **Ctrl+Shift+A** on the keyboard to open the Appointment form and fill out the appropriate fields.

2. To assign a category, click the `Categories...` button.

3. In the **Available Categories** list, select the category you want to assign.

4. Click the `OK` button to return to the Appointment form.

5. Finish filling out the Appointment form, and then click the `Save and Close` button.

## Edit an Appointment

1. Open the existing appointment by double-clicking on the appointment on the Calendar.

2. Make changes to the information on the Appointment form.

3. When you are finished, click the `Save and Close` button on the Appointment toolbar.

## Move an Appointment

1. From the Calendar folder, locate the appointment you want to move.

2. Drag the appointment to a new time or date on the schedule, and drop it in place.

---

**TIP**

If you want the appointment to keep the same time, but need to move it to a new date, you can drag the appointment from the schedule and drop it onto the new date on the Date Navigator.

---

## Delete an Appointment

1. From the Calendar folder, select the appointment you want to delete by clicking on it.

2. Click the `X` button on the Outlook toolbar.

> **TIP**
>
> You also can right-click on the appointment and choose **Delete** from the shortcut menu to remove the appointment from your schedule.

**Print an Appointment**

1. To print an appointment's details from the Calendar, first select the appointment.

2. Right-click on the appointment and choose **Print** or click the **Print** 🖨 button on the Outlook toolbar.

> **TIP**
>
> You can also print appointment details from the appointment form. Just click the **Print** 🖨 button on the Appointment toolbar.

*See Also* Calendar, Print, Reminder

## ARCHIVE

To help remove clutter and restore disk space, archive items you no longer need to access, such as old email messages. You can archive old items manually or let AutoArchive do it for you. When you archive items, they are removed from their current folder and moved to an archive file.

**Set Up AutoArchive**

1. Choose **Tools, Options** to open the Options dialog box.

2. Select the **Other** tab and click the [ AutoArchive... ] button to open the AutoArchive dialog box.

**3.** Select the **AutoArchive Every** check box and then specify the number of days between archives.

**4.** If you want to be prompted before archiving items, click the **Prompt Before AutoArchive** check box.

**5.** If you want expired items moved to the Deleted Items folder after they reach their expiration date, click the **Delete Expired Items When AutoArchiving** check box.

**6.** To specify an archive file to store items in instead of Outlook's default archive file, click the Browse ... button, select the folder and filename, and click the OK button.

**7.** Click the OK button to return to the Options dialog box.

**8.** Click the OK button again to exit the Options dialog box.

### Set Up AutoArchive Properties for a Folder

**1.** Right-click the folder on the Outlook Bar and select **Properties**. This opens the Properties dialog box.

**2.** Select the **AutoArchive** tab, and enable the **Clean Out Items Older Than** check box.

**3.** Designate the value in months, weeks, or days when items are to be archived automatically.

**4.** Outlook stores the archived items in a default archive folder, but you can choose another folder, if needed. Click the Browse ... button and select another archive folder. Then click the OK button.

**5.** Click the OK button to exit the Properties dialog box.

---

**TIP**

Outlook saves the archive folder as a .pst file type, which indicates a personal folder. Personal folders are typically located on your computer's hard disk drive rather than on a network server. This means you can access the folder at any time, and compact or archive it as necessary to save space on your computer.

### Perform a Manual Archive

1. To manually archive a folder, choose **File, Archive**.
2. To archive all the folders, choose **Archive All Folders According to Their AutoArchive Settings**.
3. To archive one folder, choose **Archive This Folder and All Subfolders**, and then select the folder.
4. Use the **Archive Items Older Than** drop-down list to set a limit to the archive items. Items dated before the date specified will be archived automatically.
5. Click the [ OK ] button to exit.

*See Also* Customize Outlook

### ATTACHMENT
see Email    pg 40

## AUTODIALER

Use your computer's modem to dial the phone numbers of contacts in Outlook's Contacts list. Instead of wasting time trying to find a phone number or memorizing it yourself, let Outlook take care of it. After the number is dialed, pick up the receiver to start talking or use your computer's microphone (if applicable).

### AutoDial a Contact

1. Open the Contacts folder (click the [icon] button on the Outlook Bar) and select the contact you want to call.
2. Click the **AutoDialer** [icon] button on the Outlook toolbar to open the New Call dialog box.
3. Click the **Number** drop-down arrow and select which number you want to dial (such as business, home, or mobile).

Click here to choose a number.

**4.** To use Outlook's Journal feature to create a journal entry that documents the call, enable the **Create New Journal Entry When Starting New Call** check box.

**5.** Click the `Start Call` button to have your modem dial the number.

**6.** After the **Call Status** changes to **Connected**, pick up the receiver to talk, or use your computer's microphone, depending on your setup.

**7.** When your conversation is finished, click the `End Call` button.

**8.** Click the `Close` button to close the dialog box.

---

**TIP**

To view details about a contact, click the `Open Contact` button in the New Call dialog box.

---

### Add a Number to the Speed Dial List

**1.** Click the icon on the Outlook Bar to open the Contacts folder.

**2.** Click the **AutoDialer** button on the Outlook toolbar to open the New Call dialog box.

**3.** Click the `Dialing Options...` button to open the Dialing Options dialog box.

**4.** Enter the person's name in the **Name** text box.

**5.** Click inside the **Phone Number** text box and type the phone number.

**6.** Click the `Yes` button to add the number to the speed dial list.

**7.** Click the `OK` button to close the Dialing Options dialog box.

**8.** Click the `Close` button to close the New Call dialog box.

### Dial a Number from the Speed Dial Menu

**1.** Click the Contacts icon on the Outlook Bar to open the Contacts folder.

2. Click the **AutoDialer** ⌾ drop-down arrow on the Outlook toolbar and choose **Speed Dial**.

3. Select the number you want to dial.

4. Click the `Start Call` button to have your modem dial the number.

5. After the **Call Status** changes to **Connected**, pick up the receiver to talk, or use your computer's microphone.

6. When your call is finished, click the `End Call` button.

7. Click the `Close` button to close the dialog box.

---

**TIP**

To change the way your modem dials, click the `Dialing Properties...` button in the New Call dialog box to open the Dialing Properties dialog box, where you can make changes to your modem's settings.

---

*See Also* Contacts, Journal

## AUTOPREVIEW

Outlook's AutoPreview feature lets you view the first few sentences of an email message from the Inbox. This enables you to check the contents of the message before opening it, which is particularly handy if you receive a lot of junk email. This feature differs from the Preview pane, which lets you to view the message from the Inbox in a separate pane. AutoPreview is also available in the Tasks folder (which lets you see task details) and the Deleted Items folder.

### Turn On AutoPreview

1. Switch to the Inbox by clicking the **Inbox** button: ⌨.

2. Choose **View**, **AutoPreview**.

---

**TIP**

You can also find the **AutoPreview** command on the **View** menu when using the Tasks or Deleted Items folders.

---

Preview a message before opening it.

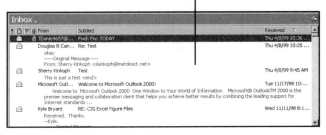

**Turn Off AutoPreview**

1. Switch to the Inbox ( ![] ), Tasks ( ![] ), or Deleted Items ( ![] ) folders.
2. Open the **View** menu and deselect **AutoPreview**.

*See Also* Deleted Items, Email, Views

## BLIND CARBON COPY
see Email   pg 40

# CALENDAR

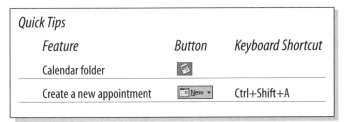

Quick Tips

| Feature | Button | Keyboard Shortcut |
|---|---|---|
| Calendar folder | | |
| Create a new appointment | New ▼ | Ctrl+Shift+A |

Use the Calendar to track your daily schedule, whether it includes appointments, events, or tasks. The Calendar can help you keep organized and on top of each day's activities. By default, Calendar first opens in Day view, but you can change your view as needed.

**Change Calendar Views**

1. Click the **Calendar**  button on the Outlook Bar to open the Calendar folder.

20

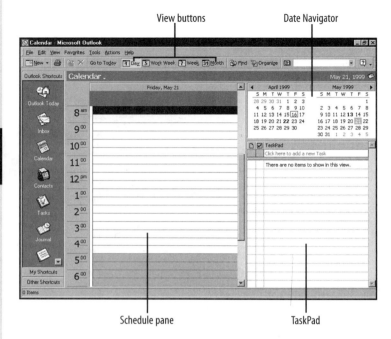

2. To view your Calendar by a typical workweek (five days), click the **Work Week** button.

3. To view your Calendar by week (seven days), click the **Week** button.

4. To view your Calendar by month, click the **Month** button.

5. To view your Calendar by day, click the **Day** button.

> **TIP**
> To change the size of a Calendar pane, such as the Schedule pane, move the mouse pointer over the pane border until it takes the shape of a double-sided arrow. Then click and drag the pane to a new size.

### Select a Date with the Date Navigator

1. Click the **Calendar** button on the Outlook Bar to open the Calendar folder.

2. To display a specific date on the Calendar, click the date or week on the Date Navigator.

3. To change the months displayed on the Date Navigator, click the **Back** ⬅ or **Forward** ➡ arrow button.

Dates with appointments appear in bold.

> **TIP**
> To quickly return to today's date, click the `Go to Today` button on the Outlook toolbar.

> **TIP**
> If you drag across several days or weeks on the Date Navigator, the schedule will reflect the days you select.

*See Also* Appointments, Event, Tasks

## CARBON COPY
see Email   pg 40

# CATEGORIES

Use categories to help you track related items in Outlook, making it easy to find, sort, and filter items. You can keep track of business items by assigning the Business category to appointments, tasks, contacts, or journal entries that are related to your business, for example. You also can add your own categories to group items related to a specific project.

## 22

### View Categories

1. To view Outlook items by category, open the **View** menu from any Outlook folder (except the Inbox) and choose **Current View**, **By Category**.

### Assign a Category

1. Double-click on the Appointment, Contact, Task, or Journal you want to assign a category to. This opens the appropriate form for the item you previously created. You can also assign a category to a new item you create.
2. To assign a category, click the `Categories...` button to open the Categories dialog box.
3. In the **Available Categories** list, select the category you want to assign.

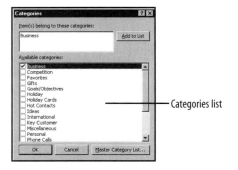
Categories list

4. To assign additional categories, select them from the list.
5. Click the `OK` button to return to the form.
6. Finish filling out the form.

### Add a New Category

1. Click the `Categories...` button to open the Categories dialog box from the Appointment, Contact, Task, Journal, or Note form.
2. Click inside the **Item(s) Belong to These Categories** text box and type a name for the category.

3. Click the [Add to List] button and the new category name is immediately added to the list.

4. Click the [OK] button to close the Categories dialog box.

---

**TIP**

Depending on which Outlook folder you have open, you can also access the Categories dialog box through the Edit menu. Choose **Edit**, **Categories**.

---

### Delete a Category

1. Click the [Categories...] button to open the Categories dialog box from the Appointment, Contact, Task, Journal, or Note form.

2. From the Categories dialog box, click the [Master Category List...] button to open the Master Category List dialog box.

3. Select the category you want to delete.

4. Click the [Delete] button.

5. Click the [OK] button to return to the Categories dialog box.

6. Click the [OK] button again to exit the dialog box.

*See Also* Organize

## CHANGE FOLDERS
see Outlook Bar    pg 95

## CLOSE OUTLOOK
see Exit Outlook    pg 51

## COMPOSE A MESSAGE
see Email    pg 40

## CONTACTS

> *Quick Tips*
>
> | Feature | Button | Keyboard Shortcut |
> |---|---|---|
> | Open the Contacts folder | | |
> | Add a new contact | New | Ctrl+Shift+C |

Outlook can help you organize the names, addresses, email addresses, and phone numbers of the people you contact the most. The Contacts folder lists your contacts as miniature address cards, and you easily can add more or edit existing contacts as needed. The information for each contact also is available in the Outlook Address Book. The easiest way to add a contact is to use the Contact form.

### Add a Contact

1. Open the Contacts folder and click the New button on the Outlook toolbar or press **Ctrl+Shift+C** on the keyboard. This opens the Contact form where you can add a new contact.

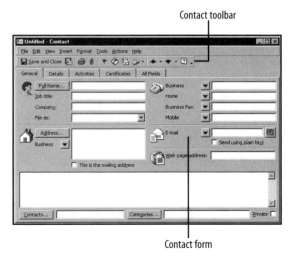

Contact toolbar

Contact form

2. On the **General** tab, enter name, address, and phone information (press **Tab** to move from field to field).

3. Optional: Use the phone number field's drop-down arrows to change the field's description, if needed. For example, if you click the **Business** drop-down arrow, a list of other phone number descriptions appears and you can choose another description for the phone number.

4. To enter additional information, such as birth date or spouse name, select the **Details** tab.

5. To continue entering more contacts, click the **Save and New** button on the Contact toolbar to save the contact and open a new Contact form.

6. When you are finished entering contact information, click the Save and Close button.

---

**TIP**

To add a contact who works for the same company as the contact you're viewing, open the **Actions** menu on the Contact form and choose **New Contact from Same Company**. This option saves you from having to type the same information, such as the address, for each contact.

---

### Assign a Category to a Contact

1. Open the Contact form (press **Ctrl+Shift+C**) and fill out the appropriate fields.

2. To assign a category, click the Categories... button.

3. In the **Available Categories** list, select the category you want to assign.

4. Click the OK button to return to the Contact form.

5. Finish filling out the Contact form, and then click the Save and Close button.

### Change the Contacts View

1. By default, the Contacts folder lists your contacts as miniaturized address cards. To change the display, click the Contacts icon on the Outlook Bar to open the Contacts folder.

**26**

2. Choose **View, Current View,** and select a view option from the submenu, such as **Detailed Address Cards** or **Phone List**.

### Edit a Contact

1. Double-click on the contact in the Contacts folder.

2. Make changes to the information on the Contact form.

3. When you are finished, click the 🖫 Save and Close button on the Contact toolbar.

---

**TIP**

To view different contacts while using the Contacts form, click the **Previous Item** 🔺▾ and **Next Item** 🔻▾ buttons to move back and forth between contact records.

---

### Delete a Contact

1. From the Contacts folder, select the contact you want to delete by clicking it.

2. Click the **Delete** ✖ button on the Outlook toolbar.

---

**TIP**

You can also right-click on the contact and choose **Delete** from the shortcut menu to remove it from your Contacts list.

---

### Print Contact Information

1. To print contact details from the Contacts folder, right-click the contact and choose **Print**.

### Find a Contact

1. Click the 🔍Find button on the Outlook toolbar.

2. Enter the name of the person you're looking for in the **Look For** text box.

3. Click the Find Now button or press **Enter**.

## TIP

You can quickly navigate the contents of your Contacts folder with the Find feature by typing in the first few letters of the contact you're looking for; then press **Enter**.

### Import Contacts

1. From the Outlook window, choose **File, Import and Export**.

2. The first Import and Export Wizard dialog box appears. Choose the import action you want to take, such as **Import from Another Program or File**. Click the [ Next > ] button to continue.

3. Select the type of program you're importing from. (If you're importing a vCard, you won't see this step.)

4. Locate and double-click the file you want to import.

5. Choose where you want the contact information imported to; in most cases, the Outlook Contacts folder is fine.

6. Click the [ Finish ] button to complete the import.

### Export Contacts

1. From the Outlook window, choose **File, Import and Export**.

2. In the first Import and Export Wizard dialog box that appears, select **Export to a File** and click the [ Next > ] button to continue.

3. Select the type of export file you want to create, such as an **Access Database** or a **Comma Separated Values** file type; click the [ Next > ] button to continue.

4. Select the **Contacts** folder to export your contact information from and click the [ Next > ] button.

5. Choose where you want the data exported to; use the [ Browse ... ] button to locate a folder, and then click the

[OK] button to return to the wizard. Click the [Next>] button to continue.

6. Click the [Finish] button to complete the export.

*See Also* Address Book, Find an Outlook Item, vCards, Views

## COPY ITEMS

*Quick Tips*

| Feature | Keyboard Shortcut |
| --- | --- |
| Copy command | Ctrl+C |
| Paste command | Ctrl+V |

You can copy an Outlook item between folders by using the Copy command on the Edit menu and then pasting the item into the folder you want to copy it to. You can also copy text from one form field to another. Outlook uses the same Copy and Paste commands found in other Windows programs. In addition, you also can copy an item to make it into a new item type. For example, drag a contact from the Contacts folder over to the Note icon on the Outlook Bar to create an instant note using the contact's information.

**Copy an Item with the Copy Command**

1. Select the item you want to copy. For example, if you want to copy an email message from the Inbox into another email folder, first select the message. To select more than one message at a time, hold down the **Ctrl** while clicking on the messages.
2. Choose **Edit**, **Copy**, or press [Ctrl]+[C].
3. Open the folder you want to copy the item to.
4. Choose **Edit**, **Paste**, or press [Ctrl]+[V].

**TIP**

To copy like items, such as messages or tasks, from one folder to another folder that holds the same type of item, use the preceding steps. You also can copy an item from one place in the list to another. For example, you can copy a task in the Tasks folder and place the copy at the end of the list of tasks.

**TIP**

You can copy text from one form field to another. Simply select the text you want to copy and choose **Edit, Copy** from the form's menu bar. Then click in the field where you want the text copied to and select **Edit, Paste**.

### Copy an Item by Dragging and Dropping

1. Select the item you want to copy.

2. Hold down the **Ctrl** key and drag the item to the Outlook Bar and drop it into the appropriate folder. This copying technique works best for copying items between same-type folders. For example, you might copy a project-related email message into a Project folder that holds similar email messages.

**TIP**

If you drag an item to a folder that uses another item type, Outlook assumes you want to create a new item and opens the appropriate form. For example, if you drag a contact item from the Contacts folder and drop it on the Notes icon on the Outlook Bar, Outlook assumes you want to create a new note based on the contact information.

### Copy a Contact into a Meeting Request

1. Select the contact you want to copy in the Contacts folder.

2. Drag the contact to the Outlook Bar and drop it into the Calendar folder.

3. A Meeting form opens with information copied from the contact. Add details about the appointment, such as a date and time, and click [Send ▼] to send the email invitation.

4. Click the [Close] button to exit the Meeting form.

### Copy a Task into an Appointment

1. Select the task you want to turn into an appointment.

2. Drag the task from the Tasks list and drop it on the Calendar icon 📆 on the Outlook Bar.

3. An Appointment form opens with relevant information from the task details filled in. Fill out the rest of the form details, as needed.

4. Click the [Save and Close] button on the Appointment form toolbar to save and close the form.

### Copy a Contact into an Email Message

1. Select the contact you want to copy into an appointment.

2. Drag the contact from the Contacts list and drop it on the Inbox icon 📧 on the Outlook Bar.

3. An email Message form opens with relevant information from the contact entered. Fill out the rest of the message details, as needed.

4. Click the [Send ▼] button on the Message form toolbar to send the message to the Outbox.

*See Also* Move Items

## CUSTOMIZE OUTLOOK

You can use several methods to customize the way Outlook looks and acts. You can use larger icons or change how items appear in each folder, for example. Use the Options dialog box to change items specific to a folder, or use the Customize dialog box to change the toolbars and menu commands. The Options dialog box also has general options you can change that affect the entire program.

### Set Larger Icons

1. If you prefer larger toolbar buttons and icons, choose **Tools, Customize**.

2. Select the **Options** tab.

3. Enable the **Large Icons** check box.

4. Click the [ Close ] button to exit the Customize dialog box.

### Turn On/Off Personalized Menus

1. Use Outlook's personalized menus to display the commands you use the most. Choose **Tools, Customize**.

2. Select the **Options** tab.

3. Place a check mark in the **Menus Show Recently Used Commands First** check box to turn the feature on, or deselect an existing check mark to turn it off.

4. Click the [ Close ] button to exit the Customize dialog box.

### Customize Menu Commands

1. Use the Customize dialog box to specify which commands appear or don't appear on the Outlook menus. Choose **Tools, Customize** to open the Customize dialog box and turn on Customize mode.

2. To remove a command from any menu, display the menu while the Customize dialog box appears onscreen, and then simply drag the command off the menu.

3. To add a command to a menu, first open the menu where you want to insert a new command.

4. Click the **Commands** tab in the Customize dialog box and select the command you want to add (scroll through the list of command categories—each category lists a different set of commands). Drag the command from the **Commands** list box and drop it on the menu where you want it added.

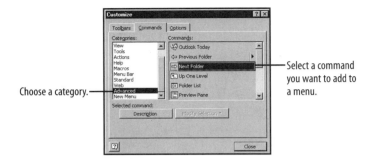

Choose a category.

Select a command you want to add to a menu.

5. To save your changes, click the Close button.

> **TIP**
>
> If it turns out you don't like all the changes you made to the menu commands, you can return your Outlook menus to their original state. Reopen the Customize dialog box, click the **Toolbars** tab, select **Menu Bar** and click the Reset... button. Click the OK button when prompted about the changes, and then click the Close button to exit the Customize dialog box.

**Customize the Toolbar**

1. Choose **Tools, Customize** to open the Customize dialog box. You're now in Customize mode and can make changes to the toolbar.

2. To remove a button from the toolbar, simply drag it off the toolbar.

3. To add a new button to the toolbar, select the **Commands** tab in the Customize dialog box and locate the category and command you want to add.

Command categories

Drag the command from this list to the toolbar.

4. Drag the button from the **Commands** list onto the toolbar.

5. Click the [ Close ] button to exit the Customize dialog box and save your changes.

---

**TIP**

You can always return your toolbar to its original settings after customizing it. Open the Customize dialog box, select the toolbar on the **Toolbars** tab, and click the [ Reset... ] button. Click the [ OK ] button when prompted about the changes, and then click the [ Close ] button to exit the Customize dialog box.

---

### Customize Email Features

1. Choose **Tools, Options** to display the Options dialog box.

2. From the **Preferences** tab, click the [ E-mail Options... ] button to open the E-Mail Options dialog box.

3. Change the message handling options in the upper portion of the dialog box by enabling or disabling the appropriate check boxes.

4. Change how replies and forwards are handled in the lower portion of the dialog box.

5. To change the default settings for saved messages or importance levels, click the [ Advanced E-mail Options... ] button to open the Advanced E-Mail Options dialog box.

6. Make any changes, as necessary. Then click the [ OK ] button to return to the E-Mail Options dialog box.

7. To change email message tracking options, click the [ Tracking Options... ] button on the E-Mail Options dialog box.

8. Use the Tracking Options dialog box to change tracking settings, and then click the [ OK ] button to return to the E-Mail Options dialog box.

9. Click the [ OK ] button to close the E-Mail Options dialog box.

10. Click the [ OK ] button to close the Options dialog box.

**34**

### Change Mail Delivery Options

1. If you're using Outlook in Internet Only mode, you can change the mail delivery options. Choose **Tools**, **Options** to display the Options dialog box.

2. Select the **Mail Delivery** tab.

3. Use the **Mail Account** options to change how Outlook sends and receives email messages.

4. Use the **Dial-Up** options to change how Outlook connects to your Internet account.

5. Click the ⬛ OK button to close the Options dialog box.

### Change Mail Services Options

1. If you're using Outlook in Corporate/Workgroup mode, you can change the mail services options. Choose **Tools**, **Options** to display the Options dialog box.

2. Select the **Mail Services** tab.

3. Use the **Startup Settings** options to change which profile is used.

4. Use the **Mail Options** area of the tab to change which service is used for your email.

5. Click the ⬛ OK button to close the Options dialog box.

### Change Mail Format Options

1. Choose **Tools**, **Options** to display the Options dialog box.

2. Select the **Mail Format** tab.

3. Use the **Message Format** options to change how others view your email messages, such as in plain text or Outlook Microsoft Rich Text (which includes formatting).

4. To add a signature (a line of personalized text) to your email messages, select a signature from the drop-down list at the bottom of the tab.

5. Click the ⬛ OK button to close the Options dialog box.

### Customize an Email Signature

1. Choose **Tools, Options** to display the Options dialog box.

2. Select the **Mail Format** tab.

3. Click the [ Signature Picker... ] button to open the Signature Picker dialog box.

4. Click the [ New... ] button to open the Create New Signature dialog box.

5. Type a name for the signature and click the [ Next > ] button.

6. Enter the text you want to include as your signature. You also can format the text, as needed.

7. When you are finished, click the [ Finish ] button to exit the Edit Signature dialog box.

8. Click the [ OK ] button to close the Signature Picker dialog box.

9. To use the signature you just created, be sure it's displayed in the **Use This Signature by Default** box (if it's not, click the drop-down arrow and select it from the list).

10. Click the [ OK ] button to close the Options dialog box.

### Customize Calendar Features

1. Choose **Tools, Options** to display the Options dialog box.

2. From the Preferences tab, click the [ Calendar Options... ] button to open the Calendar Options dialog box.

3. Select the Calendar Work Week check boxes to specify which days of the week appear in your workweek display.

4. To change which day you want to be the first day of the week, click the **First Day of Week** drop-down arrow and change the setting.

**36**

5. To change your schedule's start and end times on the Calendar's Schedule pane, click the **Start Time** and **End Time** drop-down arrows and change the settings.

6. If you're using Outlook on a network, click the `Free/Busy Options...` button to change how your Free/Busy information is displayed (click the `OK` button to return to the Calendar Options dialog box).

7. After making changes to the Calendar options, click the `OK` button.

8. Click the `OK` button again to close the Options dialog box.

### Customize Task Features

1. Choose **Tools, Options** to display the Options dialog box.

2. From the Preferences tab, click the `Task Options...` button to open the Task Options dialog box.

3. To change the color of overdue tasks as they appear on the TaskPad, click the **Overdue Tasks** drop-down arrow and choose another color.

4. To change the color of completed tasks, click the **Completed Tasks** drop-down arrow and choose a new color.

5. When you are finished, click the `OK` button to close the Task Options dialog box.

6. Click the `OK` button again to close the Options dialog box.

### Customize Contact Features

1. Choose **Tools, Options** to display the Options dialog box.

2. On the Preferences tab, click the `Contact Options...` button.

**37**

3. Use the Contact Options dialog box to change how contacts are listed by default in the Contacts list based on name.

4. When you are finished, click the [ OK ] button.

5. Click the [ OK ] button again to close the Options dialog box.

### Customize Journal Features

1. Choose **Tools, Options** to display the Options dialog box.

2. On the Preferences tab, click the [ Journal Options... ] button to open the Journal Options dialog box.

3. From the **Automatically Record These Items** list box, specify which Outlook items to record as journal entries. Select an item to enable its check box.

4. From the **For These Contacts** list box, select which contacts to record journal entries for. Select an item to enable its check box.

5. From the **Also Record Files From** list box, select which items you want to include from other Office files with your journal entries.

6. The **Double-Clicking a Journal Entry** options let you specify which action a double-click will take when performed on a journal entry. Choose an action.

7. Click the [ AutoArchive Journal Entries... ] button to open the Journal Properties dialog box, where you can set how often journal entries are archived.

8. Click the [ OK ] button when you are finished.

9. Click the [ OK ] button to return to the Options dialog box.

10. Click the [ OK ] button again to close the Options dialog box.

### Customize Note Features

1. Choose **Tools, Options** to display the Options dialog box.

2. On the Preferences tab, click the [ Note Options... ] button to open the Note Options dialog box.

3. Click the **Color** drop-down arrow and choose a new background color for your notes.

4. Click the **Size** drop-down arrow to specify a new notes size.

5. To change the font for notes, click the [ Font... ] button and specify another font, size, or font color; then click the [ OK ] button.

6. When you are finished, click the [ OK ] button to exit the Notes Options dialog box.

7. Click the [ OK ] button again to exit the Options dialog box.

### Change the Startup Folder

1. Choose **Tools, Options**.

2. Select the **Other** tab.

3. Click the [ Advanced Options... ] button.

4. Click the **Startup in This Folder** drop-down arrow and choose another folder from the list.

5. When you are finished, click the [ OK ] button.

6. Click the [ OK ] button again to exit the Options dialog box.

*See Also* Archive, AutoPreview, Calendar, Contacts, Email, Journal, Notes, Preview Pane, Tasks

## DATE NAVIGATOR
see Calendar    pg 19

# DELETED ITEMS

*Quick Tips*

| Feature | Button |
|---------|--------|
| Deleted Items folder | 🗑 |

The Deleted Items folder acts as a holding area for any Outlook item you delete. Instead of permanently deleting an item, Outlook gives you a chance to review the item before removing it for good. You also can set up Outlook to automatically delete items from the Deleted Items folder when you exit the program, saving you from having to do it yourself.

**Delete Items**

1. Click the **Deleted Items** 🗑 icon on the Outlook Bar to open the Deleted Items folder.

2. Select the item you want to permanently delete from the Deleted Items list box. To select more than one item at a time, press Ctrl while selecting items. To select every item in the list, press **Ctrl+A** on the keyboard.

3. Click the **Delete** ☒ button on the Outlook toolbar.

4. Confirm the deletion by clicking the Yes button.

---

**TIP**

To delete the contents of an entire folder, choose **Tools, Empty "Deleted Items" Folder**.

---

**Automatically Empty the Deleted Items Folder When Exiting**

1. Choose **Tools, Options**.

2. Select the **Other** tab.

3. Enable the **Empty the Deleted Items Folder upon Exiting** check box.
4. Click the `OK` button.

*See Also* Folder List

### DRAFT
see Email   pg 40

## EMAIL

| Quick Tips | | |
|---|---|---|
| Feature | Button | Keyboard Shortcut |
| Inbox | 📧 | Ctrl+Shift+I |
| Send/Receive Mail | Send/Receive | Alt+C |
| Create a New Message | New | Ctrl+Shift+M |
| Reply to a Message | Reply | Ctrl+R |
| Reply to All | Reply to All | Ctrl+Shift+R |
| Forward a Message | Forward | Ctrl+F |
| Read the Previous Message | ⬆ | Ctrl+. |
| Read the Next Message | ⬇ | Ctrl+, |

Use Outlook to send, receive, and manage your email messages. The Inbox folder keeps track of every message you receive, and you can preview a message before opening it by using the Preview Pane or Outlook's AutoPreview feature. The Outbox folder stores all your outgoing messages until you're ready to send them. Use the Message form window to compose and reply to messages, add file attachments, set priority levels, and even format your message text.

### Check for New Mail

1. Click the **Inbox** icon on the Outlook Bar or press **Ctrl+Shift+I** to open the Inbox.
2. Click the **Send/Receive** button on the Outlook toolbar, or press (Alt)+(C) on the keyboard to check for new mail messages.
3. Outlook logs you on to your Internet account and collects any email messages you have waiting. Outlook then logs off and displays any messages in your Inbox.

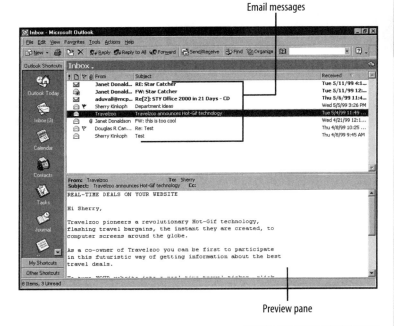

Email messages

Preview pane

### TIP

To change which mail account you need to use to check your email, choose **Tools**, **Send/Receive**. Then select the account you want to check for mail messages.

**Preview a Message with AutoPreview**

1. Click the **Inbox** icon on the Outlook Bar or press **Ctrl+Shift+I** to open the Inbox.
2. To preview the first few lines of a message without opening the message as a separate window, choose **View, AutoPreview**.

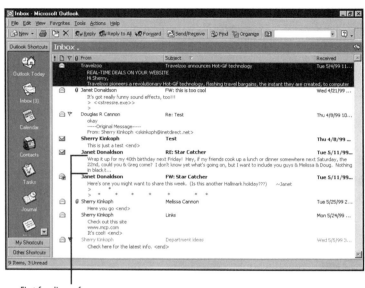

First few lines of a message

> **TIP**
> To turn AutoPreview off again, choose **View, AutoPreview**.

**Preview a Message with the Preview Pane**

1. Click the **Inbox** icon on the Outlook Bar or press **Ctrl+Shift+I** to open the Inbox.
2. To preview the message's entire content without opening a separate message window, choose **View, Preview Pane**.

> **TIP**
> To close the Preview Pane, choose **View, Preview Pane**.

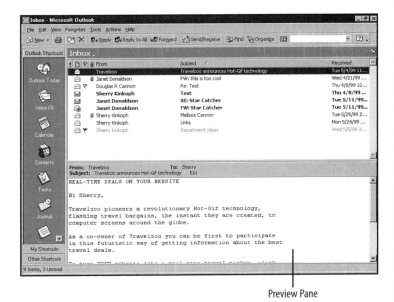

Preview Pane

### Read a Message

1. Click the **Inbox** icon on the Outlook bar to open the Inbox.
2. To read a message listed in your Inbox list, double-click on the message. The message opens in its own message window.
3. To exit a message window, click the window's **Close** button.

> **TIP**
> Use the **Previous Item** and **Next Item** buttons to move back and forth between messages. Or press Ctrl+. or Ctrl+, on the keyboard.

### Reply to a Message

1. Select the message you want to reply to.
2. Click the **Reply** button on the Message form's toolbar, or press Ctrl+R on the keyboard.
3. The message sender's name appears in the **To** text box. To enter your reply text, just start typing.

**44**

4. To send the reply, click the [Send ▾] button on the Message form's toolbar.

---

**TIP**

To reply to everyone on the sender's To list (that is, everyone who received the message), click the [Reply to All] button on the Message form's toolbar or press Ctrl+↑Shift+R on the keyboard.

---

### Forward a Message

1. Select the message you want to forward.
2. Click the [Forward] button on the Message form's toolbar.
3. Inside the **To** text box, enter the email address of the person you want to forward the message to. Or use the [To...] button to select an address from your Address Book.
4. Click the [Send ▾] button on the Message form's toolbar to send the message to Outlook's Outbox.

### Send a Message from the Outbox

1. To send any messages you have waiting in the Outbox, log onto your Internet account and click the [Send/Receive] button on the Outlook toolbar or press Alt+C on the keyboard.

### Mark a Message As Read or Unread

1. Click the **Inbox** icon on the Outlook Bar to open the Inbox.
2. Select the message you want to mark.
3. Right-click on the message and choose **Mark As Unread** or **Mark As Read**.

### Delete a Message

1. Click the **Inbox** icon on the Outlook Bar to open the Inbox.
2. Select the message you want to remove and click the **Delete** ☒ button on the Outlook toolbar. Or right-click on the message and choose **Delete**.

### Compose a New Message

1. Press Ctrl+◆Shift+M on the keyboard. Or, from any Outlook folder, click the **New** button's drop-down arrow on the Outlook toolbar and choose **Mail Message** from the list. A new Message form window opens.

2. Inside the **To** text box, enter the email address of the recipient—you can enter as many addresses as you want. (If needed, use the **Cc** box to add carbon copy recipients.)

---

**TIP**

If you type in an email address, you can check it against the Address Book by clicking the Check Names ▣ button on the Message form toolbar. The Check Names feature is turned on by default and automatically checks names you type in the To and Cc text boxes against your Address Book. If this feature is turned off, however, you can check names manually.

---

3. Click inside the **Subject** text box and give the message a title.

4. Click inside empty message area and type your message text.

5. Click the ▣Send ▾ button to send the message to Outlook's Outbox.

---

**TIP**

To add an email address from the Address Book, click the ▣To▸ button in the Message form, select a name from the list, and then click the ▣To▸ button. Click the OK button to return to the Message form window.

---

### Carbon Copy a Message

1. From the Message form window, fill out the message details as you normally would. Then, to carbon copy the message to another person (or other people), click inside the **Cc** text box and enter the appropriate email address(es).

**2.** To carbon copy someone from your Address Book, click the `Cc...` button, select a name, and click the `Cc...` button again. Click the `OK` button to return to the Message form.

### Blind Carbon Copy a Message

**1.** From the Message form window, fill out the message details, such as main recipient and subject. Then, to blind carbon copy someone, which means the message is also sent to another party without the To recipient's knowledge, choose **View, Bcc Field**. A **Bcc** text box then is added to the Message form.

**2.** To fill in the Blind Carbon Copy field, click inside the **Bcc** text box and enter the email address of the person you want to send a blind carbon copy to.

**3.** To blind carbon copy someone from your Address Book, click the `Bcc...` button, select a name, and click the `Bcc...` button again. Click the `OK` button to return to the Message form.

### Format Message Text

**1.** To assign text formatting to your email message text, open the **View** menu and change the message format to **HTML** or **Rich Text**. (You cannot add text formatting to messages composed in Plain Text format.)

---

**TIP**

HTML format can include features such as numbering, ruled lines, backgrounds, and other formatting associated with Web pages. Rich Text format can include only text formatting, bullets, and alignment. Plain text format is exactly as its name implies: plain, no-frills text.

---

**2.** Select the message text you want to format.

**3.** Use the buttons on the Formatting toolbar in the Message form window to change the text format. To view additional Formatting toolbar buttons, click the **More Buttons** `»` button.

**47**

---

**TIP**

To see both the Standard and Formatting toolbars in the
Message window in their entirety, choose **Tools**, **Customize**.
Then disable the **Standard and Formatting Toolbars Share
One Row** check box on the Options tab. Click the [ Close ]
button to exit the dialog box.

---

### Draft a Message

1. To save a message you're composing without sending it
   yet, open the Message form window's **File** menu and
   choose **Save**.

2. The file is saved and stored in the Drafts folder. Click
   the Message form's **Close** ☒ button to close the form
   window.

3. To open the message again, click the [ My Shortcuts ] group
   button on the Outlook Bar to open the **My Shortcuts**
   group. Then click the [ Drafts ] icon and double-click the
   message.

### Create a Message from a Contact

1. Open the Contacts folder and select the contact you
   want to send a message to, and then click the **Send
   Message to Contact** [ ] button on the Outlook toolbar.

2. Fill out the message subject and text.

3. Click the [ Send ▾ ] button, and the message is sent to
   the Outbox.

---

**TIP**

Another way to send a contact a message is to right-click over
the contact and choose **New Message to Contact**.

---

### Change Message Priority and Sensitivity

1. To change a message's sensitivity settings and delivery
   options, click the [ Options... ] button in the Message form
   window.

2. Click the **Importance** drop-down arrow to assign an
   importance level (**Low**, **Normal**, **High**) to the message.

**48**

Change the level using these drop-down arrows.

Click here to be notified when your message is read.

3. Click the **Sensitivity** drop-down arrow to set a sensitivity level (**Normal**, **Personal**, **Private**, **Confidential**).

4. Use the **Delivery Options** settings to change whom the message reply is sent to, to change where the copy of the sent message is saved, and to set delivery dates.

5. Use the **Tracking Options** section to request a read receipt to notify you when the person receives the email message. Enable the **Request a Read Receipt for This Message** check box.

6. Click the ⬚ Close button to exit the dialog box and apply any changes.

---

**TIP**

Not all email servers/clients will allow a read receipt request, so keep this in mind when expecting a read receipt from the recipient.

---

### Sort Out Junk Email

1. To sort a message as junk email, select the email you consider junk email from the Inbox list.

2. Right-click on the message and choose **Junk E-Mail**, **Add to Junk Senders List**.

3. The sender's name is added to your junk email list.

### Move Junk Email to the Junk Email Folder

1. From the Inbox folder, click the [Organize] button on the Outlook toolbar to open the Organize pane.

2. Select the **Junk E-Mail** tab.

3. Click the first drop-down arrow and select **Move**. Then click the [Turn on] button. This option moves any junk email you receive from your Inbox to the Junk E-Mail folder, where you can view or delete it at another time.

4. To close the Organize pane, simply open another Outlook folder or click the **Close** [×] button.

*See Also* File Attachment, Flag for Follow Up, Format, Rules Wizard, Signature, Stationery

## EVENT

Not all items you add to your Outlook schedule are appointments. Some items are events. A *calendar event* is any activity that lasts the entire day or doesn't have a specific time, such as an anniversary, conference, vacation, or birthday. Use events in your daily calendar to block off larger time slots than appointments. Events appear as banners at the top of the schedule date.

### Schedule an Event

1. Click the **Calendar** [icon] icon on the Outlook Bar to open the Calendar folder.

2. Choose **Actions, New All Day Event**. The Event form window opens.

3. Fill in the details pertaining to the event. Start by filling in a title for the event in the **Subject** text box and entering a location in the **Location** text box.

4. Use the **Start Time** and **End Time** drop-down lists to specify a time frame or date range for the event.

5. Enable the **All Day Event** check box (this option is what makes an event different from a regular appointment).

# 50

6. After you fill in the Event details, click the [⊞ Save and Close] button on the Event toolbar. The event now appears as a banner at the beginning of the day in the Schedule pane (use Day view to see it clearly).

### Edit an Event

1. Click the **Calendar** 📅 icon on the Outlook Bar to open the Calendar folder.

2. Double-click on the event you want to edit.

3. Make any changes to the details in the Event form window.

4. Click the [⊞ Save and Close] button to exit the window and apply the new changes.

### Set a Recurring Event

1. Click the **Calendar** 📅 icon on the Outlook Bar to open the Calendar folder.

2. Double-click on the event you want to make into a recurring event.

3. Click the [↻ Recurrence...] button on the Event form's toolbar.

4. Use the options in the Appointment Recurrence dialog box to set a recurrence pattern (**Daily**, **Weekly**, **Monthly**, **Yearly**), or range.

5. After you set the recurrence options, click the [ OK ] button to return to the Event form window.

6. Click the [⊞ Save and Close] button to exit the Event form window.

### Delete an Event

1. From the Calendar folder, right-click on the event you want to delete and choose **Delete** from the shortcut menu.

*See Also* Calendar, Reminder

## EXIT OUTLOOK

You can exit the Outlook program in several ways. Use the method that best suits your work needs. Unlike other Office programs, there's no need to save your work before exiting. Any of the following methods will work:

- Click the program window's **Close** ☒ button.
- Choose **File, Exit**.
- Press (Alt)+(F4) on the keyboard.

### EXPORT

see Address Book   pg 4

see Contacts   pg 24

## FAVORITES

Outlook's Favorites menu and the Favorites folder (found in the Other Shortcuts group on the Outlook bar) keep a running list of your favorite Web sites as marked in your Web browser, as well as favorites files and folders. To quickly view a page without leaving the Outlook program window, simply select the favorite page from the list.

### Open a Favorite Web Page

1. Open the **Favorites** menu and select the Web page you want to view.

2. The page appears in Outlook. (If you're not logged on to your Internet account, use the Logon dialog box to connect to your account first.)

### Add a Favorite

1. As you're viewing Web pages from Outlook, you might run across another page you want to mark as a favorite. Display the page in the Outlook program window.

2. Choose **Favorites, Add to Favorites**. The Add to Favorites dialog box opens.

3. Use the default page name, or type a new name in the **File Name** text box.
4. Click the [Add] button. The page is added to the Favorites list that appears in the Favorites menu as well as the Favorites folder.

*See Also* Web Page

## FILE ATTACHMENT

You can attach files of any type to Outlook email messages. The recipient can open the file from within the message or save the file to open later. Keep in mind, however, that the recipient *must* have the appropriate program to view the file.

### Attach a File to an Email Message

1. Use the Message form window to compose and address your email message.
2. From the Message form window, click the **Insert File** button on the Message toolbar to open the Insert File dialog box.
3. Double-click on the file you want to attach.
4. The file attachment appears as an icon in the Message form window and will be sent with the message.

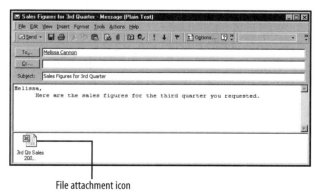

File attachment icon

**53**

---

**TIP**

To select more than one file to attach from the Insert File dialog box, press Ctrl while selecting files. Then click the [ Insert ▼ ] button to insert the files into the email message.

---

### Save a File Attachment

1. Open the message containing the file attachment.

2. Right-click on the attachment icon and choose **Save As** to open the Save As dialog box.

3. Locate and open the folder you want to save the file to.

4. Use the **File Name** text box to assign another name, or leave the existing name as is.

5. Click the [ 🖫 Save ] button, and the file is saved to your hard drive.

### Open a File Attachment

1. Open the message containing the file attachment.

2. Double-click the file attachment icon. Depending on which program was used to create the file, the corresponding program on your computer opens so that you can view the file.

*See Also* Email, QuickView

## FILE MANAGEMENT

Use Outlook to manage your computer files and folders as well as items you create and store in Outlook. You can view and open files from your hard drive or from a floppy disk.

### View Files on My Computer

1. Click the [ Other Shortcuts ] group button on the Outlook Bar.

2. Click the **My Computer** 🖳 icon.

3. Double-click the drive you want to view.

4. Double-click the folder you want to open.

## TIP

If you're using Outlook on a network, you might need to connect to your network drive. Display the **Other Shortcuts** group on the Outlook Bar and click the **My Computer** 🖳 icon. Choose **Tools, Map Network Drive**. Choose the drive you want to use and enter the path to the folder you want to connect to. Then click the [ OK ] button.

### View Files in the My Documents Folder

1. Click the [ Other Shortcuts ] group button on the Outlook Bar.
2. Click the **My Documents** 🏠 icon.

## TIP

Use the **View** menu to change how you look at files and folders in My Computer and My Documents.

### Open a File from Outlook

1. To open a file from the list of folders and files in My Computer or My Documents, double-click the filename.
2. The program associated with the file immediately opens and displays the file.

*See Also* Folder List, Views

# FIND

Considering the many items Outlook can help you track and organize, you might need help locating a specific item from time to time. Use the Find tool to assist you. Selecting this tool opens a separate pane at the top of the Outlook folder you're using, such as the Inbox or Contacts folder. From the Find pane, you can enter the item text you want to locate, and Outlook looks for the item for you.

### Find an Outlook Item

1. From any of Outlook's main feature folders (Inbox, Calendar, Contacts, Tasks, Journal, Notes), click the [ 🔍 Find ] button on the Outlook toolbar.

2. Enter the name of the item you're looking for in the **Look For** text box, or enter any keyword located in the item's title or subject matter.
3. Click the `Find Now` button or press ↵Enter.
4. Click the Find pane's **Close** ⊠ button to close the pane when finished. Or, simply open another Outlook folder.

**Advanced Find**

1. From any of Outlook's main feature folders (Inbox, Calendar, Contacts, Tasks, Journal, Notes), click the `Find` button on the Outlook toolbar.
2. Click the `Advanced Find...` button in the upper-right corner of the Find pane to open the Advanced Find dialog box.

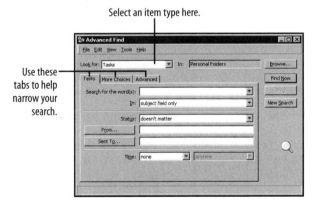

Select an item type here.

Use these tabs to help narrow your search.

3. Click the **Look For** drop-down arrow and choose the type of Outlook item you want to search for.
4. The first tab in the dialog box varies, based on the type of Outlook item you select in step 3. If you select the message item, for example, the first tab is **Messages**. The tabs have options for narrowing your search, such as searching in certain fields or searching for a particular time or date.
5. Use the **More Choices** tab to find more options for narrowing your search, such as searching for an item of a particular category.

6. Use the **Advanced** tab to enter search criteria, such as conditions and values.
7. Click the [Find Now] button to start a search.
8. Outlook displays the search results at the bottom of the Advanced Find dialog box. To open an item from the list, double-click on the item.
9. To close the Advanced Find dialog box, click the **Close** ☒ button.

> **TIP**
> If the first search doesn't reveal the results you are looking for, try again. Click the [New Search] button in the Advanced Find dialog box and enter new search criteria.

## FLAG FOR FOLLOW UP

*Quick Tips*

| Feature | Button | Keyboard Shortcut |
|---|---|---|
| Flag for Follow Up | 🚩 | Ctrl+Shift+G |

Outlook can help you remember important tasks, such as replying to an email message or following up on an important phone call. The Flag for Follow Up feature works with email messages and contacts. When a Flag for Follow Up icon is assigned to a message or a contact, you'll be reminded about the item with a Reminder prompt box.

### Flag a Message for Follow Up

1. From the Inbox folder, select the message you want to flag.
2. Right-click on the message and choose **Flag for Follow Up**. The Flag for Follow Up dialog box appears.
3. Click the **Flag To** drop-down arrow and select an action from the list.

4. Click the **Due By** drop-down arrow and select a due date for the followup.

5. Click the `OK` button, and the message is flagged with a tiny flag icon in the Inbox list. You'll be reminded about the followup when the date/time approaches.

### Flag a Contact for Follow Up

1. From the Contacts folder, select the contact you want to flag.

2. Right-click on the contact and choose **Flag for Follow Up**. The Flag for Follow Up dialog box appears.

3. Click the **Flag To** drop-down arrow and select an action from the list.

4. Click the **Due By** drop-down arrow and select a due date for the followup.

5. Click the `OK` button, and the contact is flagged. You'll be reminded about the followup when the date/time approaches.

### Clear a Follow Up Flag

1. Right-click on the flagged item and choose **Clear Flag** from the shortcut menu.

### Mark a Flagged Item As Completed

1. Double-click on the flagged item to open the item in its own window.

2. Click the **Flag for Follow Up** [▼] button on the form window's toolbar to display the Flag for Follow Up dialog box.

3. Select the **Completed** check box.

4. Click the `OK` button to exit the Flag for Follow Up dialog box.

*See Also* Reminder

## FOLDER

*Quick Tips*

| Feature | Keyboard Shortcut |
|---|---|
| Create a New Folder | Ctrl+Shift+E |

Outlook has features for managing folders, including folders on your computer's hard drive. You can easily create new folders, change folder names, or delete folders from within the Outlook program window.

### Create a New Folder

1. Choose **File, Folder, New Folder**. Or press [Ctrl]+[Shift]+[E] on the keyboard. The Create New Folder dialog box opens.

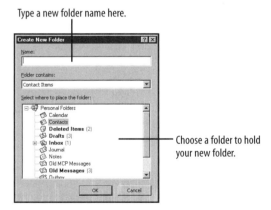

Type a new folder name here.

Choose a folder to hold your new folder.

2. Inside the **Name** text box, enter a folder name.
3. Use the **Folder Contains** drop-down arrow to select the type of Outlook item you want the folder to hold.
4. Select a folder where you want to store the new folder.
5. Click the [ OK ] button to create the folder and exit the Create Folder dialog box.

**6.** Outlook prompts you to add a shortcut icon for the folder to the Outlook bar. Click the [ Yes ] button to add the icon, or click the [ No ] button to skip this step.

> **TIP**
>
> To create a new folder directly in Outlook's Folder List, first select a folder to hold the new folder. Right-click on the folder and choose **New Folder** from the shortcut menu. The Create New Folder dialog box opens.

### Delete a Folder

1. Choose **View, Folder List**.

2. Select the folder you want to delete.

3. Right-click on the folder, and choose **Delete** from the shortcut menu.

4. Click the [ Yes ] button to confirm the deletion.

### Rename a Folder

1. Choose **View, Folder List**.

2. Select the folder you want to rename.

3. Right-click on the folder, and choose **Rename** from the shortcut menu.

4. Enter a new name and press (↵Enter).

### View Your Computer's Folders and Files from Outlook

1. Click the [ Other Shortcuts ] group button on the Outlook Bar to display the Other Shortcut icons.

2. Click the **My Computer** 🖳 icon to display the My Computer folders and files.

3. Click the **My Documents** 📁 icon on the Outlook bar to view the contents of the My Documents folder.

4. Click the **Favorites** 📁 icon on the Outlook bar to view the Favorites shortcuts.

*See Also* Folder List

## FOLDER LIST

The Folder List displays each Outlook folder, subfolders, and individual items in each folder. The Folder List is arranged in the same hierarchy as your computer's hard drive.

### View the Folder List

1. Choose **View, Folder List**. Or click the **Folder** drop-down arrow next to the current folder name.

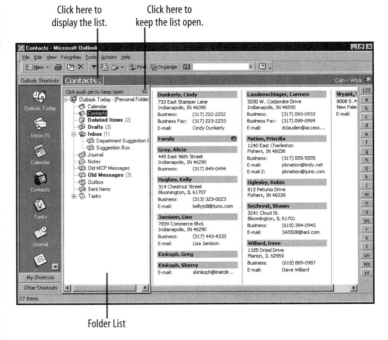

Folder List

2. To keep the Folder List displayed, click the **Push Pin** button in the upper-right corner of the list.
3. To view a folder's contents, select the folder from the Folder List.

## FORM

Outlook uses forms to allow user input. Forms are used to compose email messages, set appointments, tasks, and so on. You can customize Outlook's forms and make changes to the fields and design of the forms.

### Design a Form

1. Choose **Tools, Forms, Design a Form** to open the Design Form dialog box.
2. Select the form you want to change.
3. Click the [Open] button. The form opens in Design mode.
4. You can now make changes to the form's fields, field positions, text, and more.
5. To exit the form after making changes, click the form window's **Close** ☒ button.

> **TIP**
>
> For more information about designing forms, see Que's *Special Edition Using Microsoft Outlook 2000*, ISBN 0-7897-1909-6.

## FORMAT

You can choose from three types of message formats in Outlook: Plain Text (the default), Rich Text, and HTML. Plain Text format is the most universal format for Internet email. If you know that the person you're emailing to has Outlook or another email reader program that reads text formatting, though, you can use Rich Text or HTML format. These two formats enable you to format your message text, such as changing font and styles.

*Quick Tips*

| Feature | Keyboard Shortcut |
|---|---|
| Switch to Plain Text | Ctrl+Shift+O |
| Start a New Message | Ctrl+Shift+M |

## Change the Message Format

1. To start a new message, press Ctrl+⬆Shift+M on the keyboard.

2. To change the message format, open the Message form's **Format** menu and change the message format to **Plain Text**, **HTML**, or **Rich Text**. (Plain Text is selected by default.)

3. The message format you chose now appears in the Message form's title bar, along with the subject of the message.

> **TIP**
>
> When you reply to a message, the reply is formatted in the same message format as the message you received. You can change the format, if necessary, but keep in mind that the recipient might not be able to read the message in another format.

## Set a Default Format

1. Choose **Tools, Options** to display the Options dialog box.

2. Select the **Mail Format** tab.

3. Click the **Send in This Message Format** drop-down arrow and choose a message format: **Plain Text**, **HTML**, or **Rich Text**.

4. Click the ⬛ OK ⬛ button to close the Options dialog box.

> **TIP**
>
> To change which encoding language is used for international email messages you send, click the [International Options...] button on the Mail Format tab of the Options dialog box. Then change the language setting as needed.

*See Also* Customize Outlook, Email

## FORWARD A MESSAGE
see Email     pg 40

# GO TO

*Quick Tips*

| Feature | Button | Keyboard Shortcut |
|---------|--------|-------------------|
| Go To command | Go to Today | Ctrl+G |

The Go To command helps you locate a date in Outlook's Calendar or Journal. You also can use Go To to open a specific Outlook folder or even launch your Web browser.

### Go To Today

1. From the Calendar folder, click the Go to Today button on the Outlook toolbar to quickly view the current day on the schedule.

### Go To Date

1. Press Ctrl+G or click the Go to Today button to open the Go To Date dialog box.

2. Enter the date you want to view or click the **Date** drop-down arrow and choose a date from the pop-up calendar.

3. Optional: Use the **Show In** drop-down arrow to select a view.

4. Click the OK button.

### Go To Folder

1. Choose **View, Go To**.

2. From the submenu that appears, select a specific folder you want to open.

### Go To Web Browser

1. Choose **View, Go To**.

2. From the submenu that appears, select **Web Browser**.

## GROUP BUTTONS

see Outlook Bar    pg 95

## HELP

| Quick Tips |         |                   |
|------------|---------|-------------------|
| Feature    | Button  | Keyboard Shortcut |
| Help       | [?]     | F1                |
| What's This? |       | Shift+F1          |

Whenever you need additional assistance with using Outlook, consult the program's Help system, which includes the Office Assistant and a database of help topics. If the Help system doesn't produce the information you're looking for, you can visit Microsoft's Web site for additional help.

### Ask the Office Assistant

1. Press (F1) or click the **Microsoft Outlook Help** [?] button on the Outlook toolbar to display the Office Assistant.
2. Click inside the text box in the Office Assistant balloon and type in the question text. The question text can be a complete sentence, a single word, or a phrase.
3. Click **Search** or press (↵Enter).
4. The Office Assistant produces a list of possible topics for you to choose from. Click a topic that most closely matches the information you want. A Help window detailing the information opens.

**65**

5. Read the information and, if needed, click on any links to view related information.

6. When you are finished, click the window's **Close** ☒ button to close the Help window.

---

**TIP**

If the question you typed didn't produce the results you expected, try entering keywords associated with the topic you're interested in.

---

### Hide the Office Assistant

1. To close the Office Assistant completely, choose **Help, Hide the Office Assistant**.

   **or**

1. Right-click over the Office Assistant character and choose **Hide** from the shortcut menu.

---

**TIP**

By default, the Office Assistant moves out of your way as you work. If you're new to Outlook, you might want to leave the Assistant open to help you as you try new features.

---

### Customize the Office Assistant

1. Click the **Options** button in the Office Assistant balloon to open the Office Assistant dialog box.

2. Select the **Gallery** tab and choose another character using the [< Back] or [Next >] button.

3. Click the [OK] button after choosing another character.

### Change Office Assistant Settings

1. Click the **Options** button in the Office Assistant balloon.

2. Select the **Options** tab in the Office Assistant dialog box to change which options are turned on or off.

3. Change the settings as needed, and then click the [OK] button to exit and apply the changes.

### Turn Off Office Assistant's Sounds

1. From the Office Assistant balloon, click the **Options** button, or right-click over the Assistant and choose **Options** from the shortcut menu.

2. Select the **Options** tab.

3. Deselect the **Make Sounds** check box.

4. Click the ⬚ OK ⬚ button.

### Turn Off the Office Assistant

1. By default, the Office Assistant appears whenever you access help. To turn it off, display the Assistant, and then click the **Options** button.

2. Deselect the **Use the Office Assistant** check box on the Options tab.

3. Click the ⬚ OK ⬚ button to exit the dialog box.

4. The next time you want to use the Help database, press (F1).

---

**TIP**

To bring back the Office Assistant after turning it off, choose **Help, Show the Office Assistant**.

---

### Turn On Outlook's Tip of the Day

1. From the Office Assistant balloon, click the **Options** button, or right-click over the Assistant and choose **Options** from the shortcut menu.

2. Select the **Options** tab.

3. Click the **Show the Tip of the Day at Startup** check box to place a check mark in the box.

4. Click the ⬚ OK ⬚ button. The next time you start Outlook, you're presented with a useful tip for using the program.

### Navigate the Help Window

1. Click the **Show** button on the Help window toolbar to view the Help tabs.
2. Click the **Back** button to view the previous help information.
3. Click the **Forward** button to return to the help topic you were viewing before you clicked the **Back** button.
4. Click the **Hide** button to hide the Help tabs.
5. Click the **Close** button to close the Help window.

> **TIP**
> Click the **Options** button on the Help window toolbar to view a list of additional Help options.

### Look Up a Topic in Help Contents

1. From the Help window, select the **Contents** tab.
2. Double-click a book icon to open a list of topics.

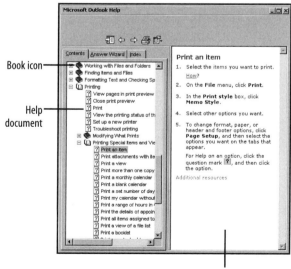

Book icon

Help document

View the topic here.

3. Some topics have subtopics; keep double-clicking the book icons to list all the documents available.

4. To view a topic, double-click on the topic. This displays the information in the right side of the Help window.

### Ask the Answer Wizard

1. From the Help window, select the **Answer Wizard** tab.

2. Click inside the **What Would You Like to Do?** text box and enter the word or phrase you want help with.

3. Click the [ Search ] button or press (↵Enter).

4. A list of related topics appears in the bottom portion of the Answer Wizard tab. To view a topic, click on it.

### Look Up a Term in the Help Index

1. From the Help window, select the **Index** tab.

2. Click inside the **Type Keywords** text box and enter the word you want to look up.

3. Click the [ Search ] button or press (↵Enter).

4. A list of related topics appears in the bottom portion of the Index tab. To view a topic, click on it.

---

**TIP**

To start a new search, click the [ Clear ] button and look up another word.

---

### Print a Help Topic

1. To print a topic from the Help window, click the **Print** 🖨 button on the Help toolbar. This opens the Print dialog box.

2. Make any necessary changes to the print options, and then click the [ OK ] button to print the topic.

### Help on the Internet

1. Choose **Help, Office on the Web**.

2. If you're not logged onto the Internet, connect to your Internet account now; click the [ Connect ] button.

**69**

3. Your Web browser opens to Microsoft's Web site to the Outlook page. Follow the Assistance link to find help with the Outlook product.

4. When finished, close the browser window and log off your Internet account.

**What's This?**

1. To find quick information about an onscreen element, choose **Help, What's This?**

2. The mouse pointer takes the shape of a question mark. Click the onscreen element you want to know more about, such as a toolbar button or dialog box option. A pop-up box appears offering details about the feature.

3. Click anywhere onscreen or press Esc to close the help information.

## HOLIDAYS
see Event    pg 49

## IMPORT
see Address Book    pg 4

see Contacts    pg 24

## INBOX

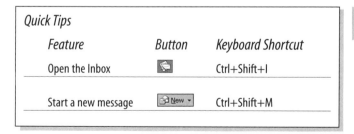

*Quick Tips*

| Feature | Button | Keyboard Shortcut |
|---|---|---|
| Open the Inbox |  | Ctrl+Shift+I |
| Start a new message | New | Ctrl+Shift+M |

The Inbox folder stores email messages you send and receive. You can quickly view messages you've received

**70**

and see who sent the message and the date it arrived in your mailbox. You can also see priority levels and file attachments assigned to messages from the Inbox folder.

### Change the Inbox View

1. Open the Inbox folder; Click the **Inbox** 📧 icon on the Outlook Bar or press **Ctrl+Shift+I** on the keyboard.

2. Choose **View, Current View**; then select a view you want to use from the submenu.

### Sort Inbox Messages

1. Open the Inbox folder; click the Inbox 📧 icon on the Outlook Bar or press **Ctrl+Shift+I** on the keyboard.

2. Click on the column label of the column you want to sort. For example, to sort the messages alphabetically according to the name of the sender, click the **From** column label.

---

**TIP**

Another way to sort a column is to right-click over the column label and choose **Sort Ascending** or **Sort Descending** from the shortcut menu.

---

### Customize Inbox Columns

1. Open the Inbox folder; click the **Inbox** 📧 icon on the Outlook Bar or press **Ctrl+Shift+I** on the keyboard.

2. Right-click on a column label and choose **Format Columns** from the shortcut menu. The Format Columns dialog box opens.

3. Select the column you want to format from the **Available Fields** list box.

4. To change the label of the colum, click inside the **Label** text box and enter a new label.

5. To change the width of the column, click inside the **Specific Width** text box and enter the number of characters for the column width.

6. To change the alignment of the column, select a new alignment from the **Alignment** options.

7. When finished, click the [ OK ] button to exit the dialog box and apply any changes.

---

**TIP**

Another way to change the column widths in the Inbox is to drag the column border to a new size. Hover the mouse pointer over the border of the column label you want to change. The pointer becomes a two-sided arrow. Drag the border to a new size.

---

*See Also* AutoPreview, Email, Preview Pane

## INCOMING MESSAGE
see Email    pg 40

## INTERNET
see Email    pg 40

see Web Page    pg 135

# ITEMS

Outlook helps you track everyday items, such as appointments, contacts, notes, and tasks. Each entry you make in an Outlook folder is an item. You can move and copy items between Outlook folders as well as to other programs.

### Select an Item

1. To select an item from any Outlook folder, simply click on the item.

### Open an Item

1. To open the item's form, double-click on the item.

## Copy an Item

1. Select the item you want to copy. To select more than one item at a time, hold down the **Ctrl** while clicking on the items.
2. Choose **Edit**, **Copy**, or press Ctrl+C.
3. Open the folder you want to copy the item to.
4. Choose **Edit**, **Paste**, or press Ctrl+V.

## Move an Item

1. Select the item you want to move.
2. Choose **Edit**, **Cut**, or press Ctrl+X.
3. Open the folder you want to move the item to.
4. Choose **Edit, Paste**, or press Ctrl+V.

## Delete an Item

1. Select the item you want to delete.
2. Click the **Delete** ☒ button on the Outlook toolbar or press Ctrl+D. This moves the item to Outlook's Deleted Items folder.

## Manually Archive Items

1. To manually archive a folder of items, choose **File**, **Archive** to open the Archive dialog box.
2. To archive all the folders, choose **Archive All Folders According to Their AutoArchive Settings**.
3. To archive one folder, choose **Archive This Folder and All Subfolders**, and then select the folder.
4. Use the **Archive Items Older Than** drop-down list to set a limit to the archive items. Items dated before the date specified will be archived automatically.
5. Click the ⟨ OK ⟩ button to exit the dialog box and archive the items.

*See Also* Archive, Copy Items, Deleted Items, Paste Items

# JOURNAL

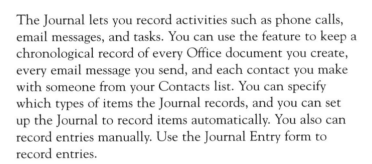

*Quick Tips*

| Feature | Button | Keyboard Shortcut |
|---|---|---|
| Journal folder | | |
| New Journal entry | New ▾ | Ctrl+Shift+J |
| Find an entry | Find | |

The Journal lets you record activities such as phone calls, email messages, and tasks. You can use the feature to keep a chronological record of every Office document you create, every email message you send, and each contact you make with someone from your Contacts list. You can specify which types of items the Journal records, and you can set up the Journal to record items automatically. You also can record entries manually. Use the Journal Entry form to record entries.

**Open the Journal**

1. Click the **Journal** icon on the Outlook Bar to open the Journal.

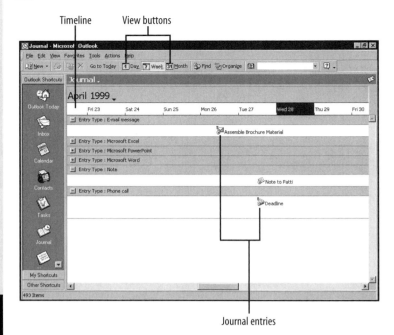

Timeline — View buttons — Journal entries

### Add a Journal Entry Manually

1. From the Journal folder, click the **New** button on the Outlook toolbar to open the Journal Entry form or press **Ctrl+Shift+J** on the keyboard.
2. Enter a subject title for the entry in the **Subject** text box.

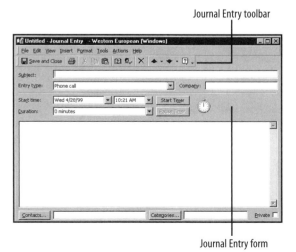

Journal Entry toolbar

Journal Entry form

3. Click the **Entry Type** drop-down arrow and choose a type, such as Phone call or Email message.
4. Optional: Use the **Company** text box to enter the name of the associated company.
5. By default, the **Start Time** fields show the current date and time. To start the timer and record the time spent on the task, click the Start Timer button, or use the **Duration** drop-down list to specify a time increment or type one in.
6. Use the notes text box to enter any notes or details about the entry.
7. Click the Contacts... button to assign a contact to the entry.
8. Click the Categories... button to assign a category to the entry.
9. To stop the timer, click the Pause Timer button.
10. Click the Save and Close button to save and close the entry. It's immediately added to the Journal.

### Set Up Automatic Journal Entries

1. Choose **Tools, Options** to open the Options dialog box.
2. From the **Preferences** tab, click the Journal Options... button.
3. Place a check mark next to all items, files, and contacts you want the Journal to record automatically.

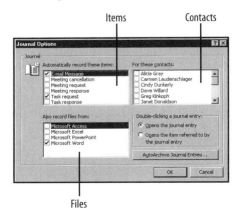

**4.** When finished, click the `OK` button.

**5.** Click the `OK` button again to exit the Options dialog box.

### Edit a Journal Entry

**1.** Double-click on the entry from the Journal folder.

**2.** Make any changes necessary to the Journal Entry form.

**3.** Click the `Save and Close` button to save your changes and exit the form.

### Delete a Journal Entry

**1.** Right-click over the Journal entry and choose **Delete**.

**or**

**1.** Select the entry and click the **Delete** `X` button on the Outlook toolbar.

### Print a Journal Entry

**1.** Open the Journal entry you want to print.

**2.** Click the **Print** button on the Entry Form toolbar.

---

**TIP**

You can also right-click over the Journal entry you want to print and choose **Print** from the shortcut menu.

---

### Change Journal Entry Views

**1.** To view your Journal entries by day in a timeline view, click the `1 Day` button on the Outlook toolbar.

**2.** To view entries by week, click the `7 Week` button.

**3.** To view entries by month, click the `31 Month` button.

**4.** To view entries by category or type, choose **View**, **Current View** and select the view you want to use.

**Find a Journal Entry**

1. From the Journal folder, click the [🕙 Find] button on the Outlook toolbar.

2. Enter the word or phrase you want to search for among your Journal entries in the **Look For** text box.

3. Click the [Find Now] button or press ↵Enter.

**AutoArchive Journal Items**

1. Right-click on the **Journal** [icon] icon on the Outlook Bar and select **Properties**. This opens the Properties dialog box.

2. Select the **AutoArchive** tab, and enable the **Clean Out Items Older Than** check box.

3. Designate the value in months, weeks, or days when items are to be archived automatically.

4. Outlook stores the archived items in a default archive folder, but you can choose another folder, if needed. Click the [Browse ...] button and select another archive folder. Then click the [💾 OK] button.

5. Click the [OK] button to exit the Properties dialog box.

*See Also* AutoDialer, Categories, Contacts

# KEYBOARD SHORTCUTS

*Quick Tips*

| *Feature* | *Keyboard Shortcut* |
|---|---|
| Shortcut to menu command | (Alt)+underlined menu letter |

Use keyboard shortcuts to quickly activate menu commands and perform other Outlook activities. You can find keyboard shortcuts for common procedures (such as Ctrl+P for Print) listed on Outlook's menus, or you can use the Alt key along with underlined letters to open menus and menu commands.

### Open a Menu Command with the Alt Key

1. Press Alt plus an underlined letter of the menu you want to display.

2. Press the underlined letter of the command you want to activate.

# LINK

You can type a Web page address in your email message, and Outlook immediately turns the text into an active link to the site. You also can copy links from other messages or documents.

### Enter a Link

1. Open the Message form; Press **Ctrl+Shift+M**.

2. Click inside the message area and type the Web page address. As soon as you type **www.** and the first charac-ter of the link you want to enter, Outlook underlines the text and sets it off in blue.

### Follow a Link

1. Open the email message containing the link.

2. Click the link to open your Web browser and display the page.

*See Also* Email, Web Page

## MAIL MESSAGE
see Email   pg 40

## MARK AS READ
see Email   pg 40

## MAXIMIZE

Use the Maximize button to maximize the window, whether it's a program window or a form window, to its fullest size, which takes up the entire screen.

### Maximize a Window

1. Click the **Maximize** 🔲 button.

*See Also* Minimize, Restore

## MEETING

| Quick Tips | |
|---|---|
| *Feature* | *Keyboard Shortcut* |
| Plan a Meeting | Ctrl+Shift+Q |

If you're using Outlook on a network, you can publish your calendar on the network and use the Plan a Meeting feature to schedule meetings with others. The feature also lets you designate any resources needed for the meeting, such as a conference room or equipment. The Plan a Meeting feature lets you invite attendees via email messages and track their responses. The Plan a Meeting feature works with Outlook's Calendar.

### Publish Free/Busy Times

1. Choose **Tools, Options** to open the Options dialog box.
2. From the **Preferences** tab, click the [Calendar Options...] button to open the Calendar Options dialog box.

3. Click the `Free/Busy Options...` button to open the Free/Busy Options dialog box.

4. Enter the number of months to publish calendar info from in the **Publish** box, and then specify how often to update the information on the server.

5. Click the **Publish My Free/Busy Information** check box and enter the server's URL where the information is to be published.

6. Click the `OK` button to return to the Calendar Options dialog box.

7. Click the `OK` button again to exit the Calendar Options dialog box.

8. Click the `OK` button to close the Options dialog box.

### Plan a Meeting

1. From the Calendar folder, choose **Actions**, **Plan a Meeting**. The Plan a Meeting dialog box opens.

2. Enter the names of the attendees in the **All Attendees** list. Click **Type Attendee Name Here** and enter the first person's name. Continue entering names on each line for as many attendees as you need.

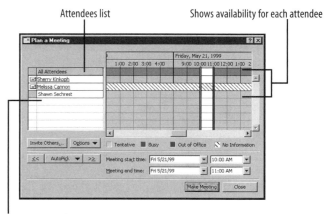

Attendees list — Shows availability for each attendee

Click here to enter an attendee name.

3. Click the **Meeting Start Time** drop-down arrows and choose a date and time for the meeting.
4. Use the **Meeting End Time** drop-down arrows to specify an end time for the meeting.
5. When you finish planning the meeting attendees and times, click the [Make Meeting] button. The Meeting form opens, which resembles the Appointment form. Refine the meeting details as needed.

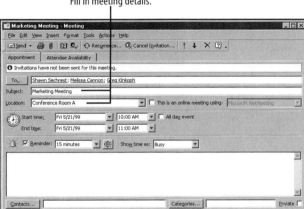

Fill in meeting details.

6. When you finish filling out the meeting details, click [Send ▼] to send email invitations to the attendees.
7. Click the [Close] button to exit the Plan a Meeting dialog box.

> **TIP**
> 
> You also can drag the green bar in the schedule area of the Plan a Meeting form to set a start time for the meeting, and drag the red bar to set an end time.

### Invite Others

1. To invite people from your current list of contacts and email addresses, click the [Invite Others...] button on the Plan a Meeting form to open the Select Attendees and Resources dialog box.

2. If the person's attendance is required, select the person's name from the list and click the [ Required -> ] button.

3. If the person's attendance is desired, but not required, select the person's name and click the [ Optional -> ] button.

4. To notify someone in charge of resources for the meeting, such as the person who schedules the conference room, select the person's name and click the [ Resources -> ] button.

5. Click the [ OK ] button to return to the Plan a Meeting form.

---

**TIP**

To plan an online meeting instead of a face-to-face meeting, enable the **This Is an Online Meeting Using** check box in the Appointment form.

---

### AutoPick a Meeting Time

1. To let Outlook find an available meeting time for the selected attendees, click the [ AutoPick ▼ ] button in the Plan a Meeting dialog box.

2. Choose an option from the list or use the arrow buttons to quickly navigate between the selected best times.

---

**TIP**

You can send a meeting request to a contact from the Contacts folder. Select the contact, and then choose **Actions, New Meeting Request to Contact**. Fill out the form and email the request to the contact.

---

### Track Responses

1. To see how the attendees are responding to your meeting invitation, open the Calendar and double-click the meeting appointment.

2. Select the **Attendee Availability** tab.

### Respond to a Meeting Request

1. Open the meeting request.

2. To accept the invitation and schedule the appointment on your calendar, click the ✓ Accept button.

3. To tentatively schedule the meeting, click the ? Tentative button.

4. To consult your calendar and check your schedule, click 🔲 Calendar... . Outlook checks your calendar and displays any conflicts and surrounding appointments.

5. To decline the invitation, click the ✗ Decline button.

6. After responding, Outlook prompts you to send the response. You can add text, if needed, pertaining to your response, and then send the response.

7. After everyone responds to your request, you can delete the meeting request from your Inbox.

*See Also* Appointments, Calendar, Deleted Items, Email

## MESSAGE
see Email    pg 40

# MINIMIZE

Use the Minimize button to reduce the window, whether it's the program window or a form window, to a button on the Windows taskbar.

### Minimize a Window

1. Click the **Minimize** 🔲 button.

*See Also* Maximize, Restore

## MOVE ITEMS

> **Quick Tips**
>
> | Feature | Keyboard Shortcut |
> |---|---|
> | Cut command | Ctrl+X |
> | Paste command | Ctrl+V |

You can move an Outlook item from one folder to another folder that stores the same type of item. Use the Cut command on the Edit menu and then paste the item into the folder you want to move it to. Outlook uses the same Cut and Paste commands found in other Windows programs.

**Move an Item with the Cut Command**

1. Select the item you want to move. For example, if you want to move an email message from the Inbox into another email folder, first select the message. To select more than one message at a time, hold down the **Ctrl** while clicking on the messages.
2. Choose **Edit, Cut,** or press Ctrl+X.
3. Open the folder you want to move the item to.
4. Choose **Edit, Paste,** or press Ctrl+V.

> **TIP**
>
> You can cut text from one form field to and place it in another with the Cut command. Simply select the text you want to copy and choosing **Edit, Cut** from the form's menu bar. Then click in the field where you want the text copied to and select **Edit, Paste**.

**Move an Item by Dragging and Dropping**

1. Select the item you want to move.
2. Drag the item to the Outlook Bar and drop it into the appropriate folder. This technique works best for moving items between same-type folders. For example, you

might move a project-related email message into a Project folder that holds similar email messages.

> **TIP**
> If you drag an item to a folder that uses another item type, Outlook assumes you want to create a new item and opens the appropriate form. If you drag a contact item from the Contacts folder and drop it on the Notes icon on the Outlook Bar, Outlook assumes you want to create a new note based on the contact information.

*See Also* Copy Items, Paste Items

## MY SHORTCUTS
see Outlook Bar   pg 95

## NET FOLDER

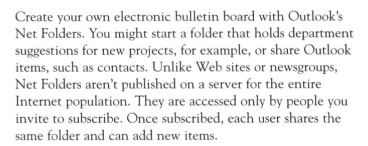

*Quick Tips*

| Feature | Keyboard Shortcut |
|---|---|
| Post to the Current Net Folder | Ctrl+Shift+S |

Create your own electronic bulletin board with Outlook's Net Folders. You might start a folder that holds department suggestions for new projects, for example, or share Outlook items, such as contacts. Unlike Web sites or newsgroups, Net Folders aren't published on a server for the entire Internet population. They are accessed only by people you invite to subscribe. Once subscribed, each user shares the same folder and can add new items.

### Create a Net Folder

1. Start by creating a new folder to be your Net Folder. Choose **File**, **New**, **Folder**.
2. Click inside the **Name** text box and give the folder a name.

3. Use the **Folder Contains** drop-down arrow to specify which Outlook items the folder will hold.

4. Click the `OK` button. You might be prompted to add a shortcut for the folder to your Outlook Bar. Click the `No` button to skip this action.

**Publish a Net Folder**

1. Open the folder you want to use as the Net Folder.

2. Choose **File**, **Share**, **This Folder** to open the Net Folder Wizard.

3. Click the `Next >` button to get started.

4. Click the `Add` button to add people you want to share the folder with.

5. From the Add Entries to Subscriber Database dialog box, select the names of the people you want to add to your subscriber list. Select a name and click the `To ->` button.

6. After you finish adding names, click the `OK` button to return to the wizard.

7. To assign a permission status, which sets up a permission level that determines what the person can do with the Net Folder, select a name from the list. Then click the `Permissions...` button.

8. Assign a permission level, and then click the `OK` button. (If the person you're inviting to subscribe doesn't have Outlook, select the Minimum permission level.)

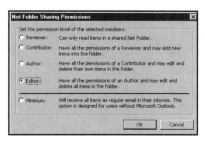

9. Click the **Next>** button to continue.
10. Enter some text that describes the type of folder you're creating and how you want the subscribers to respond. Click the **Next>** button to continue.
11. Click the **Finish** button to complete the wizard.
12. Each member will receive an email message inviting him or her to subscribe.

### Post to a Net Folder

1. Open the Net Folder you want to post to, and then choose **File, New, Post in This Folder**.
2. Click in the **Subject** box and enter a subject title for the message.
3. Click inside the note area and enter your text.
4. Click the **Post** button to post the message to the folder.

### Update a Net Folder

1. Right-click on the folder you would like to update.
2. Select **Properties**; the Properties dialog box appears.
3. Select the **Sharing** tab.
4. Click **Send Updates Now** to send out the updates.

*See Also* Email, Folder List

# NOTES

*Quick Tips*

| Feature | Button | Keyboard Shortcut |
|---|---|---|
| Notes folder | 📋 | |
| Start a New Note | New ▾ | Ctrl+Shift+N |

Outlook's Notes feature is the electronic version of yellow sticky notes you use to remind yourself of things you need to do or label papers on your desk. Use Outlook's Notes to do the same. You can attach a note to a contact, or drag a note onto the Windows desktop to remind you of an important task. You also can drag notes into other Office programs.

**Open the Notes Folder**

1. Click the **Notes** icon on the Outlook Bar to open the Notes folder.

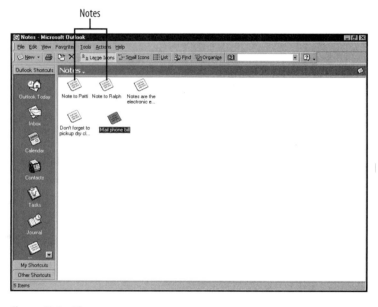

Notes

**Change Notes Views**

1. To view your notes with large icons, click the `Large Icons` button on the Outlook toolbar.
2. To view your notes with small icons, click the `Small Icons` button on the Outlook toolbar.
3. To view your notes as a list instead of icons, click the `List` button on the Outlook toolbar.

### Add a New Note

1. From the Notes folder, click the [New] button on the Outlook toolbar or press **Ctrl+Shift+N** on the keyboard.

2. Enter the note text.

3. To close the note, click **Close** ☒ in the upper-right corner of the note.

---

**TIP**

You can drag notes around the Notes folder. Just click and drag, and then drop in place.

---

### Drag a Note

1. To drag a note to the Outlook Bar, into a folder, or onto the desktop, first select the note from the Notes folder.

2. Drag the note to its new location and drop in place.

### Edit a Note

1. Double-click the note you want to edit.

2. Make changes to the note text.

3. Click **Close** ☒ to close the note.

### Resize a Note

1. Open the note.

2. Move the mouse pointer to the note border until it takes the shape of a two-sided arrow pointer ⟷ .

3. Hold down the left mouse button and drag the note border to a new size.

### Change the Note Color

1. From the Notes folder, select the note you want to color.

2. Right-click on the note, choose **Color**, and then choose the color from the list.

### Change the Note Color for All Notes

1.  To change the background color of your new notes, open the Notes folder. Then choose **Tools**, **Options**.

2.  Select the **Preferences** tab.

3.  Select the | Note Options... | button.

4.  Change the note's color using the **Color** drop-down arrow.

5.  You also can change the note's size or font, as needed.

6.  Click the | OK | button to close the Note Options dialog box.

7.  Click the | OK | button to close the Options dialog box.

### Delete a Note

1.  In the Notes folder, select the note. Then click the **Delete** ☒ button on the Outlook toolbar.

2.  You also can right-click on the Note icon from any location and choose **Delete** from the shortcut menu.

## OPEN OUTLOOK

You can open Outlook several ways. After you open Outlook, you might want to keep the program window open or minimized in order to hear and see reminder prompts for imminent appointments and tasks. You also can add Outlook to your computer's Start menu so that the program opens whenever you turn on the computer.

### Open Outlook

■ Open the **Start** menu on the Windows taskbar and choose **Programs**, **Microsoft Outlook**.

or

■ Outlook installs a shortcut icon on the Windows desktop. Double-click the **Microsoft Outlook** 🗒 icon to open the program.

**Set Up Outlook to Open Automatically**

1. Choose **Start, Settings, Taskbar & Start Menu**.

2. Select the **Start Menu Programs** tab.

3. Click the [ Add ] button to open the Create Shortcut dialog box.

4. Click the [ Browse ... ] button to open the Browse dialog box.

5. Locate the drive and folder where you installed Outlook and double-click the `Outlook.exe` file.

6. Click the [ Next > ] button to continue.

7. Select the **StartUp** folder and click the [ Next > ] button.

8. Optional: Enter a name for the shortcut, and then click [ Finish ].

9. Click the [ OK ] button to exit the Taskbar Properties dialog box. The next time you start your computer, Outlook opens automatically.

*See Also* Exit Outlook

# ORGANIZE

Use Outlook's Organize tool to help you organize items in each Outlook feature. You can use the Organize pane in the Inbox, for example, to designate where messages are stored, set rules for incoming messages, customize the way you view messages, and specify how to handle junk email. The contents of the Organize pane differ slightly among Outlook folders.

**Open the Organize Pane**

1. Click the [ Organize ] button on the Outlook toolbar.

2. To display a particular option or set of options, select the appropriate tab on the left side of the Organize pane.

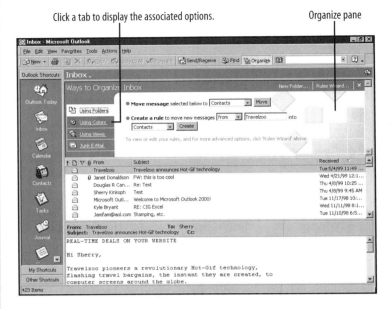

Click a tab to display the associated options.    Organize pane

### Close the Organize Pane

1. To close the Organize pane, simply open another Outlook folder or click the **Close** button.

### Organize Items into Folders

1. From the Inbox, Contacts, Tasks, or Notes folder, open the Organize pane.

2. Select the **Using Folders** tab (if it's not already displayed).

3. Use the **Move Message** option to move a selected item from the current location to another folder you designate with the drop-down arrow.

4. Click the Move button, and the item is moved.

### Organize Items into Categories

1. From the Calendar, Contacts, Journal, or Tasks folder, open the Organize pane.

2. Select the **Using Categories** tab (if it's not already displayed) to display options for organizing items by category.

**3.** To assign a category to the selected item, click the first option's drop-down arrow and select a category. Then click the `Add` button.

**4.** To start a new category, click inside the second option's text box and type a category name. Then click the `Create` button.

### Organize Items by View

**1.** From any Outlook folder, open the Organize pane.

**2.** To change the default view for those items, select the **Using Views** tab.

**3.** Select a view from the **Change Your View** list. This becomes your default view (used each time you open the feature).

### Organize Inbox Messages with Rules

**1.** From the Inbox folder, open the Organize pane.

**2.** Select the **Using Folders** tab (if it's not already displayed).

**3.** Use the **Create a Rule** option to create a new rule for automatically moving email messages from a particular person to a specified folder after the message is received. Choose a person and a folder to store the message in.

**4.** Click the `Create` button to create and apply the rule.

### Organize Inbox Messages with Colors

**1.** From the Inbox folder, open the Organize pane.

**2.** Select the **Using Colors** tab to display the Color Messages option.

**3.** Use the **Color Messages** drop-down arrows to assign a rule that applies a color to messages received from the person you specify.

**4.** Click the `Apply Color` button, and the rule is applied.

**Sort Junk Email Messages**

1. From the Inbox folder, open the Organize pane.
2. Select the **Junk E-Mail** tab to display options for coloring junk email messages you receive so that you can immediately identify them.
3. To move a message being filtered as a junk email message, click the first drop-down arrow of the option and choose **Move** from the list. Then use the second drop-down arrow to specify a folder and click the `Turn on` button.
4. To color code a junk mail message, click the first drop-down arrow of the option and choose **Color** from the list. Then use the second drop-down arrow to assign a color and click the `Turn on` button.

> **TIP**
> For additional filtering options you can assign to incoming email messages, click the **Click Here** link at the bottom of the Junk E-Mail tab in the Organize pane.

*See Also* Deleted Items, Rules Wizard, Views

### OTHER SHORTCUTS
see Outlook Bar    pg 95

## OUTBOX

*Quick Tips*

| Feature | Keyboard Shortcut |
|---|---|
| Switch to Outbox | Ctrl+Shift+O |

You can compose email messages offline and wait and send them all at once when you log on. All offline messages you compose are stored in Outlook's Outbox.

### Open the Outbox

1. Click the `My Shortcuts` group button on the Outlook Bar.
2. Click the `Outbox` icon on the Outlook Bar.

### Send Messages from the Outbox

1. From the Outbox folder, click the `My Shortcuts` button on the Outlook toolbar. Outlook logs you onto your Internet account and sends the messages. Then Outlook logs you off when it's done.

*See Also* Email

## OUTLOOK BAR

The Outlook Bar is divided into several groups. The Outlook Shortcuts group shows shortcut icons for each Outlook feature. The My Shortcuts group includes shortcuts to the Drafts, Outbox, and Sent folders; the Other Shortcuts group includes shortcuts to My Computer, My Documents, and Favorites folders. Use the group buttons to view various shortcuts and add your own shortcut icons to the group.

### View/Hide the Outlook Bar

1. Choose **View, Outlook Bar**. A check mark next to the command means the bar appears onscreen; no check mark means it's turned off.

### View a Group

1. From the Outlook Bar, click the group button representing the shortcuts you want to view.

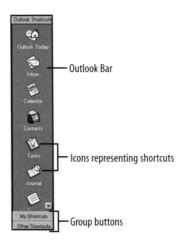

- Outlook Bar
- Icons representing shortcuts
- Group buttons

### Add a New Group

1. Right-click on the Outlook Bar and choose **Add New Group** from the shortcut menu.
2. Type a new group name.
3. Press **Enter**, and the new group button appears on the Outlook Bar.

### Delete a Group

1. Right-click over the group you want to remove and choose **Remove Group** from the shortcut menu.
2. Click the [ Yes ] button to confirm the deletion.

> **TIP**
> Deleting a group will remove all the shortcuts associated with the group.

### Rename a Group

1. Right-click over the group button you want to rename and choose **Rename Group** from the shortcut menu.
2. Type a new group name.
3. Press **Enter**, and the new name appears on the button.

### Add a Shortcut to a Group

1. Open the group where you want to place the shortcut.

2. Right-click over a blank area of the Outlook Bar and choose **Outlook Bar Shortcut**.

3. Locate and select the folder you want to add to the bar. To add a shortcut to a folder located on your hard drive, click the **Look In** drop-down arrow and choose **File System**. Then locate and select the folder.

4. Click the ⬛ OK button.

### Drag a Shortcut to a Group

1. Open the group where you want to place the shortcut.

2. Drag the shortcut, whether it's a shortcut to a program, folder, or file (including Web pages), to the Outlook Bar, and drop the shortcut when it appears where you want it.

### Delete a Shortcut from a Group

1. Right-click over the shortcut icon you want to remove and choose **Remove from Outlook Bar**.

---

**TIP**

Deleting a shortcut will not delete the actual folder or data. It merely removes the shortcut icon from the Outlook Bar.

---

### Rename a Shortcut Icon

1. Right-click over the shortcut icon and choose **Rename Shortcut**.

2. Type a new name.

3. Press **Enter**.

### Change the Shortcut Icon Size

1. To make the shortcut icons smaller, right-click on the Outlook bar and choose **Small Icons**.

2. To make the shortcut icons larger, right-click on the Outlook bar and choose **Large Icons**.

*See Also* Folder List

## OUTLOOK TODAY

You can preview each day's activities with the Outlook Today page. The page presents you with a list of the day's and week's appointments, tasks, and number of new email messages received. You can customize how the items appear on the page and make the page your default page that appears every time you open the program window.

### View the Outlook Today Page

1. Click the **Outlook Today** icon on the Outlook Bar.
2. To view any item listed on the page, click the item link.

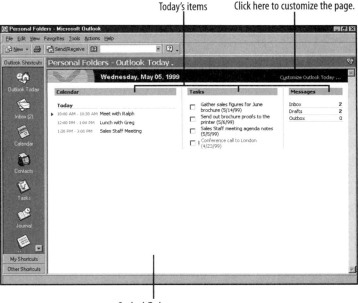

Today's items · Click here to customize the page.

Outlook Today page

### Make the Outlook Today Page the Default Page

1. Open the Outlook Today page.
2. Click the **Customize Outlook Today** button at the top of the page.
3. Enable the **When Starting, Go Directly to Outlook Today** check box.
4. Click the **Save Changes** button.

### Change the Outlook Today Page Style

1. Open the Outlook Today page.

2. Click the **Customize Outlook Today** button.

3. Click the **Show Outlook Today in This Style** drop-down arrow and choose a new style from the list.

4. Click the **Save Changes** button.

### Change the Number of Calendar Days on the Page

1. Click the **Customize Outlook Today** button on the Outlook Today page.

2. Click the **Show This Number of Days in My Calendar** drop-down arrow and choose a number.

3. Click the **Save Changes** button.

### Customize Which Tasks Appear on the Page

1. Click the **Customize Outlook Today** button on the Outlook Today page.

2. To show only the current day's tasks, click the **Today's Tasks** option button. To show every task, leave the **All Tasks** option selected.

3. To choose an order for the displayed tasks, use the **Sort My Task List By** drop-down arrow to specify an order. Then click **Ascending** or **Descending**.

4. Click the **Save Changes** button.

### Customize Which Email Messages Appear on the Page

1. Click the **Customize Outlook Today** button from the Outlook Today page.

2. Click the Choose Folders... button to open the Select Folder dialog box.

3. Click the email folders you want to display and click the OK button.

4. Click the **Save Changes** button.

*See Also* Appointments, Calendar, Email, Tasks

# 100

**PAGE SETUP**
see Print   pg 104

## PASTE ITEMS

> *Quick Tips*
>
> | Feature | Keyboard Shortcut |
> |---|---|
> | Cut command | Ctrl+X |
> | Copy command | Ctrl+C |
> | Paste command | Ctrl+V |

You can cut, copy, and paste Outlook items between folders. When you cut or copy like items between folders, such as copying an email message from the Inbox to a folder containing old messages, use the Cut, Copy, and Paste commands.

**Paste an Item**

1. Select the item you want to cut or copy. For example, if you want to copy an email message from the Inbox into another email folder, first select the message. To select more than one message at a time, hold down the **Ctrl** while clicking on the messages.
2. Choose **Edit, Copy** (or press Ctrl+C) or choose **Edit, Cut** (or press Ctrl+X).
3. Open the folder you want to copy or move the item to.
4. Choose **Edit, Paste**, or press Ctrl+V.

*See Also* Copy Items, Move Items

## PERSONAL DISTRIBUTION LIST

*Quick Tips*

| Feature | Button | Keyboard Shortcut |
|---|---|---|
| Start a New Distribution List |  | Ctrl+Shift+L |

You quickly can send the same email message to a group of people on your personal distribution list. You can have as many separate lists as you need. You easily can manage your lists, adding or deleting names as needed. Distribution lists always are marked with an icon  next to their name.

### Create a Personal Distribution List

1. From the Contacts folder, choose **Actions**, **New Distribution List**. From any other folder, choose **File**, **New**, **Distribution List**.
2. Enter a name for the list in the **Name** text box.
3. To add people from your Address Book list, click the `Select Members...` button.
4. From the Select Members dialog box, click a name you want to add to the list. Then click the `Select ->` button, or just double-click on the person's name.
5. Continue adding to the list, and click the `OK` button when finished.
6. Click the `Save and Close` button to save the list and add it to the Contacts folder by the name you assigned in step 2.

> **TIP**
>
> To update a list with any changed email addresses you've entered recently, open the list and click the `Update Now` button.

**P**102

### Add a New Name to a Personal Distribution List

1. In the Contacts folder, double-click the name of the distribution list you want to add to.

2. Click the `Add New...` button to open the Add New Member dialog box.

3. Enter the person's name and email address.

4. Click the `OK` button when finished adding names and close the Add New Member dialog box.

5. Click the `Save and Close` button to exit the Distribution List dialog box.

---

**TIP**

Use the **Notes** tab in the Personal Distribution List form to add notes about a member of the list.

---

### Remove a Name from the Personal Distribution List

1. In the Contacts folder, double-click the name of the distribution list you want to edit.

2. Select the name you want to remove.

3. Click the `Remove` button to remove the person from the list.

4. Click the `Save and Close` button to close the Distribution List dialog box.

*See Also* Address Book, Contacts, Email

### PHONE A CONTACT
see AutoDialer    pg 16

## PREVIEW PANE

The Inbox's Preview pane lets you preview an email message without having to open the entire message. This feature enables you to glance at the content and quickly skip messages you don't want to read.

### Turn the Preview Pane On or Off

1. Choose **View, Preview Pane**.

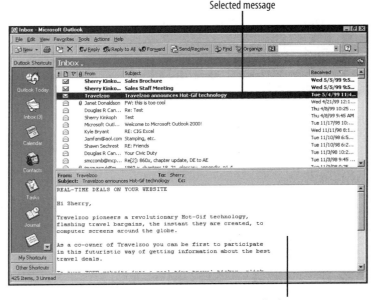

#### TIP

You can resize the Preview pane by hovering your mouse pointer between the top pane and the Preview pane until the pointer becomes a two-sided arrow. Then click and drag up or down to resize either pane.

### Customize the Preview Pane

1. Choose **Tools, Options** to open the Options dialog box.
2. Select the **Other** tab.
3. Click the [Preview Pane...] button to open the Preview Pane dialog box.
4. Use the options at the top of the dialog box to specify how messages are marked in the pane.
5. Customize the font that appears at the top of the Preview pane by clicking the [Font...] button.

6. Click the `OK` button to return to the Options dialog box.

7. Click the `OK` button again to exit the Options dialog box and apply any changes.

**See Also** Email

## PRINT

*Quick Tips*

| Feature | Button | Keyboard Shortcut |
|---|---|---|
| Print | 🖨 | Ctrl+P |
| Open Print Preview | | Ctrl+F2 |

You can print any Outlook item or list of items, and you can choose from a variety of print options. Depending on the type of Outlook item you print, you can choose from several print styles. Each style has predefined settings, such as font and margins. You can change these settings as needed. You also can preview how an item will print before you actually commit it to paper.

**Print an Item**

1. Select the item you want to print.

2. Click the **Print** 🖨 button on the Outlook toolbar or choose **File, Print**. The Print dialog box opens. (If you're printing from an open form window, choose **File, Print** to open the Print dialog box.)

3. To change the printer, click the **Name** drop-down arrow and choose another printer from the list.

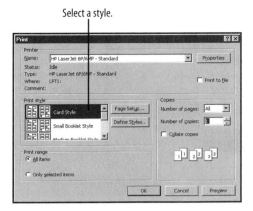

Select a style.

4. Select a print style for the item from the **Print Styles** list.

5. If printing multiple pages, use the **Number of Pages** drop-down arrow to select **All, Even,** or **Odd**.

6. To print more than one copy, click inside the **Number of Copies** text box and enter a number, or use the spin arrows to change the setting.

7. If you are printing more than one copy of several pages, enable the **Collate Copies** check box to collate the pages.

8. Use the **Print Range** options to specify a particular range for the printed item. The options here vary depending on the type of item you're printing.

9. Click the OK button to print.

> **TIP**
> To print multiple items from a list, press the (Shift) key (or press the (Ctrl) key if the items are scattered in the list) while selecting the items.

### Preview the Item with Print Preview

1. Select the item you want to preview.

2. Choose **File, Print Preview** to open the Print Preview window.

Print Preview toolbar

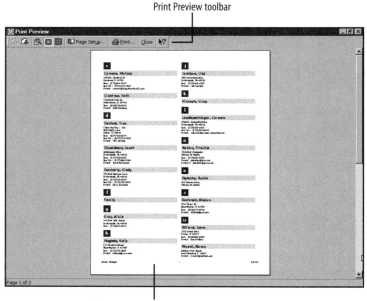

A preview of what the page will look like when printed

3. If viewing multiple pages, click the **Page Up** and **Page Down** buttons to move from page to page.

4. By default, Print Preview shows one page at a time. To view multiple pages all at once, click the **Multiple Pages** button. To return to the one-page view, click the **One Page** button.

5. To see the page at actual size, click the **Actual Size** button or click anywhere on the page. To zoom out again, click on the page.

6. To print the page as is, click the Print... button.

7. To exit Print Preview mode, click the Close button.

### Change Page Setup Options from Print Preview

1. From the Print Preview window, click the Page Setup... button to open the Page Setup dialog box.

2. Select the **Format** tab to find options for changing fonts and how sections will print.

# 107

3. Select the **Paper** tab to find options for changing paper size, type, dimensions, margins, and orientation.
4. Select the **Header/Footer** tab to find options for adding headers and footers to the printed page.
5. Click the `Print Preview` button to view the item in Print Preview mode.
6. Click the `Print...` button to print the item after making any changes.
7. Click the `OK` button to apply any changes and exit the dialog box.

### Page Setup

1. To set up how an item will print, start by selecting the item.
2. Choose **File, Page Setup**, and choose the style you want to use.
3. Make any changes to the tabs in the Page Setup dialog box. Then click the `OK` button to exit and apply the new settings.

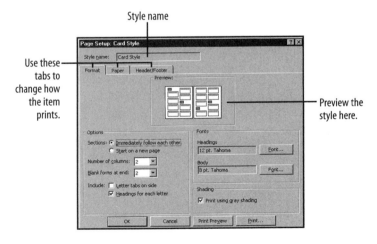

**Edit a Print Style**

1. Choose **File**, **Page Setup**, **Define Print Styles** to open the Define Print Styles dialog box.

2. Select a style and click the [ Edit... ] button to open the Page Setup dialog box.

3. Make any modifications to the style by changing the settings on the tabs, such as font or margins.

4. Click the [ OK ] button to return to the Define Print Styles dialog box.

5. Click the [ Close ] button. The next time you print using this style, the new settings are applied.

---

**TIP**

To return a style's default settings, select the style in the Define Print Styles dialog box and click the [ Reset ] button.

---

**Change Printer Properties**

1. Choose **File**, **Print** to open the Print dialog box.

2. From the Print dialog box, click the [ Properties ] button to open the Properties dialog box.

3. Select the **Paper** tab to change the paper size, source, or orientation.

4. Select the **Print Quality** tab to change the resolution.

5. Select the **Fonts** tab to change printer fonts.

6. Select the **Device Options** tab to make changes to the printer memory.

7. Click the [ OK ] button to return to the Print dialog box.

---

**TIP**

The tabs you see in the Properties dialog box will vary based on the printer you have installed. You might have similar tabs as described in the preceding steps, or your tabs might be completely different.

## QUICKVIEW

Use Outlook's QuickView feature to quickly view the contents of any file attachment. You won't be able to make changes to the file, but you can see what the file is before actually opening it.

### View a File Attachment with QuickView

1. Right-click on the file attachment icon and choose **QuickView** to open the QuickView window.
2. Click the **Close** ☒ button to close the QuickView window when finished.

### Open a File Attachment from QuickView

1. Click the **Open File** 📄 button on the QuickView toolbar.

   or

1. Choose **File, Open File for Editing**.

> **TIP**
> Depending on the type of file attached, the icon you see in step 1 will vary. This example shows a Word document icon.

## RECURRING APPOINTMENT

see Appointments   pg 9

## REDO

*Quick Tips*

| Feature | Keyboard Shortcut |
|---------|-------------------|
| Redo    | Ctrl+Y            |

Use the Redo command to immediately undo the Undo command. For example, if you deleted text in a message with the Undo command, and then decide you want it back, use the Redo command to restore it.

**110**

### Use the Redo Command

1. Choose **Edit, Redo** or press Ctrl+Y.

*See Also* Undo

## REMINDER

You can set reminders for appointments, tasks, and contacts, or even Inbox items. A *reminder* is a dialog box that appears at a preset time, along with a sound, to remind you of an upcoming engagement or activity. You can set when you want the reminder to appear and specify a sound to accompany the reminder. Outlook must be open (minimized or maximized) in order to use the Reminder feature.

### Change the Default Reminder Settings

1. Choose **Tools, Options**. The Options dialog box appears.

2. Select the **Preferences** tab.

3. To turn off the default reminder feature, deselect the **Default Reminder** check box.

4. To change the default reminder time, click the **Default Reminder** drop-down arrow and choose another time increment, or simply type in the time you want.

5. To change the default reminder for tasks, click the **Reminder Time** drop-down arrow and choose a new time or type one in.

6. Click the ___OK___ button to exit the Options dialog box and apply the new settings.

### Change Task Reminder Settings

1. Choose **Tools, Options**. The Options dialog box appears.

2. Select the **Other** tab.

3. Click the ___Advanced Options...___ button to open the Advanced Options dialog box.

P
Q
R

4. Click the [Advanced Tasks...] button to open the Reminder Options dialog box.

5. Change the Task Reminder options as needed.

6. Click the [OK] button three times to exit all the open dialog boxes and apply any changes.

---

**TIP**

The Task Reminder options affect only tasks that use due dates.

---

### Assign a Reminder to an Appointment

1. From the Appointment form, enable the **Reminder** check box.

2. Use the **Reminder** drop-down arrow to specify the length of time prior to the appointment that you want to be reminded, such as 15 minutes, or type in a time.

3. Click the [Save and Close] button to save and exit the Appointment form.

### Assign a Reminder to a Task

1. From the Task form, enable the **Reminder** check box.

2. Use the **Reminder** drop-down arrows to specify a date and hour for the reminder.

3. Click the [Save and Close] button to save and exit the Task form.

### Assign a Reminder to a Contact

1. Open the contact you want to add a reminder to.

2. From the Contact form, choose **Actions, Flag for Follow Up**. Or click the **Flag for Follow Up** [▼] button on the Contact toolbar.

3. Click the **Flag To** drop-down arrow and select a followup type.

**112**

4. Click the **Due By** drop-down arrow and choose a date on the pop-up calendar.

5. Make any necessary changes to the time, and click the [ OK ] button.

6. Click the [ Save and Close ] button to save and exit the form.

---

**TIP**

Another way to assign a reminder to a contact is to right-click on the contact and choose **Flag for Follow Up** from the shortcut menu.

---

### Change the Reminder Alarm Sound

1. Choose **Tools, Options**. The Options dialog box appears.

2. Select the **Other** tab.

3. Click the [ Advanced Options... ] button to open the Advanced Options dialog box.

4. To change the sound associated with the reminder, click the [ Reminder Options... ] button. This opens the Reminder Options dialog box.

5. Use the [ Browse ... ] button to locate and select another sound file to use, and then click the [ Open ] button to return to the Reminder Options dialog box.

6. Click the [ OK ] button three more times to exit all the open dialog boxes.

### Dismiss a Reminder

1. After the Reminder prompt box appears, click the [ Dismiss ] button.

**Postpone a Reminder**

1. From the Reminder prompt box, click the [ Snooze ] button to be reminded again in five minutes (or the time specified as the default time increment).

2. To change the next reminder time, click the drop-down arrow and choose a time increment. Then click the [ Snooze ] button.

**Open an Item from the Reminder Prompt Box**

1. From the Reminder prompt box, click the [ Open Item ] button to open the item associated with the reminder.

*See Also* Appointments, Calendar, Contacts, Tasks

## REPLY
see Email    pg 40

# RESTORE

Use the Restore button on the Outlook program window to restore the window to its previous size. Use the same button on any of Outlook's form windows to restore the form window to its previous size.

**Restore a Window**

1. Click the **Restore** [🗗] button.

*See Also* Maximize, Minimize

# RULES WIZARD

Use Outlook's Rules Wizard to help you set up actions for handling your incoming and outgoing email messages. You can set a rule that makes a prompt box appear any time you receive a priority message, for example, or automatically move messages from certain people to other folders. You can set up many types of rules, and the Rules Wizard can walk you through the procedure each time. The Rules Wizard even lists several popular rules you might want to use in addition to those you create on your own.

## Set a New Rule with the Rules Wizard

1. Open the Inbox; click the **Inbox** 📧 icon on the Outlook bar.

2. Choose **Tools, Rules Wizard**.

3. Click the `New...` button to create a new rule.

4. From the top list box, choose the type of rule you want to create.

5. Depending on the rule you select, the bottom list box displays a description of the rule and underlined values. To change a value, click the underlined value text and make your changes.

6. Click the `Next >` button to continue.

7. Specify the rule conditions, and click the `Next >` button to continue.

8. Specify what you want Outlook to do with the message, and click the `Next >` button to continue.

9. Specify any exceptions to the rule, and click the `Next >` button.

10. Enter a name for the rule, and click the `Finish` button. The rule is added to the list of rules in the Rules Wizard dialog box.

11. Click the `OK` button to exit the Rules Wizard dialog box.

## Turn a Rule On or Off

1. From the Inbox, choose **Tools, Rules Wizard**. The Rules Wizard dialog box appears.

2. Enable or disable the check box in front of the rule you want to turn on or off in the top list box. A check mark means the rule is on; no check mark means it's off.

3. Click the `OK` button to exit the Rules Wizard dialog box.

**Edit a Rule**

1. From the Inbox, choose **Tools, Rules Wizard**. The Rules Wizard dialog box appears.

2. Select the rule you want to edit.

3. To edit only the values the rule uses, click the underlined value text and change the value.

4. To edit additional settings, click the [ Modify... ] button to reopen the Rules Wizard used to create the rule.

5. Move back and forth between the Rules Wizard dialog boxes with the [ < Back ] and [ Next > ] buttons to make changes to the rule's parameters.

6. When finished, click the [ Finish ] button.

7. Click the [ OK ] button to exit the dialog box.

---

**TIP**

To run a rule immediately after you modify it, click the [ Run Now... ] button in the Rules Wizard dialog box.

---

**Delete a Rule**

1. From the Inbox, choose **Tools, Rules Wizard**. The Rules Wizard dialog box appears.

2. Select the rule you want to remove from the list box.

3. Click the [ Delete ] button.

4. Click the [ Yes ] button to confirm the deletion.

5. Click the [ OK ] button to exit the Rules Wizard dialog box.

**Rename a Rule**

1. From the Inbox, choose **Tools, Rules Wizard**. The Rules Wizard dialog box appears.

2. Select the rule you want to rename.

**116**

3. Click the `Rename...` button.

4. Enter a new name and click the `OK` button.

5. Click the `OK` button to exit the Rules Wizard dialog box.

### Import a Set of Rules

1. From the Inbox, choose **Tools**, **Rules Wizard**. The Rules Wizard dialog box appears.

2. Click the `Options...` button to open the Options dialog box.

3. Click the `Import Rules...` button to open the Import Rules From dialog box.

4. Locate and select the rules file you want to import, and then click the `Open` button.

5. Click the `OK` button to return to the Rules Wizard dialog box.

6. Click the `OK` button to close the Rules Wizard dialog box.

### Export a Set of Rules

1. From the Inbox, choose **Tools**, **Rules Wizard**. The Rules Wizard dialog box appears.

2. Click the `Options...` button to open the Options dialog box.

3. Click the `Export Rules...` button to open the Save Exported Rules As dialog box.

4. Enter a name for the file you want to export and click the `Save` button.

5. Click the `OK` button to return to the Rules Wizard dialog box.

6. Click the `OK` button to close the Rules Wizard dialog box.

*See Also* Email

# SAVE

You can save Outlook items as text files to be used with other programs, or save file attachments you receive with email messages. You also can save unfinished email messages, complete them later, and then send them at another time.

### Save a File Attachment

1. Open the message containing the file attachment.

2. Right-click on the attachment icon and choose **Save As** to open the Save As dialog box.

3. Locate and open the folder where you want to save the file.

4. Use the **File Name** text box to assign another name, or leave the existing name as is.

5. Click the [💾 Save] button, and the file is saved on your hard drive.

### Save an Item As a Text File

1. To save an Outlook item as a text file type, first select or open the item you want to save.

2. Choose **File, Save As**. The Save As dialog box opens.

3. Locate and open the folder where you want to save the item.

4. Use the **File Name** text box to give the item a name.

5. Click the **Save As Type** drop-down arrow and choose a text file type from the list, such as **Text Only**.

6. Click the [💾 Save] button, and the item is saved.

---

**TIP**

You cannot save Outlook items as document files, or other program file types. However, many programs can work with text files (TXT), so by saving the item as a text file, you will be able to use the file in another program.

---

### Save an Unfinished Email Message

1. From the message form window, choose **File, Save**.
2. The file is saved and stored in the **Drafts** folder. Click the message form's **Close** ☒ button to close the form.
3. To open the message again, click the [My Shortcuts] button on the Outlook bar to open the **My Shortcuts** group, click the [Drafts] icon, and then double-click the message.

*See Also* Customize Outlook, File Attachment, Folder List

## SCHEDULE
see Calendar    pg 19

## SEND
see Email    pg 40

## SENT ITEMS

By default, Outlook keeps a copy of every email message you send in the Sent Items folder. You can turn off this feature to save room on your computer.

### Turn Off Automatic Save

1. Choose **Tools, Options**. The Options dialog box appears.
2. Select the **Preferences** tab.
3. Click the [E-mail Options...] button to open the E-Mail Options dialog box.
4. Disable the **Save Copies of Messages in Sent Items Folder** check box.
5. Click the [OK] button to close the E-Mail Options dialog box.
6. Click the [OK] button again to exit the Options dialog box.

# SIGNATURE

A *signature* is a tag line added at the bottom of an email message you send. Signatures can be as straightforward as your name and company, or as personalized as a favorite quote. You can store as many signatures as you want in Outlook. You also can choose to include your signature with every message, or just certain messages you send.

### Create a New Signature

1. Choose **Tools, Options** to display the Options dialog box.

2. Select the **Mail Format** tab.

3. Click the [Signature Picker...] button to open the Signature Picker dialog box.

4. Click the [New...] button to open the Create New Signature dialog box.

5. Type a name for the signature and click the [Next >] button.

6. Enter the text you want to include as your signature. You also can format the text, as needed.

7. When finished, click the [Finish] button to close the Edit Signature dialog box.

8. Click the [OK] button to close the Signature Picker dialog box.

---

**TIP**

To apply the signature immediately after creating it, be sure it's displayed in the **Use This Signature by Default** list box in the Options dialog box (if it's not, click the drop-down arrow and select it from the list).

---

### Insert a Signature

1. From the email message form window, click where you want the signature to go.

2. From the message form, choose **Insert, Signature**. Then click on the signature you want to use, or click the 🖃 button on the message form's toolbar.

**120**

---

**TIP**

If the signature you want to insert is not listed on the **Signature** submenu, click **More** and then select the signature you want to use. Click the [ OK ] button to exit the dialog box and insert the signature.

---

### Automatically Insert a Signature

1. Choose **Tools**, **Options** to open the Options dialog box.
2. Select the **Mail Format** tab.
3. Click the **Use This Signature by Default** drop-down arrow and select a signature.
4. Click the [ OK ] button to exit the Options dialog box. The signature now will be added automatically to each email message you create.

### Edit a Signature

1. Choose **Tools**, **Options** to open the Options dialog box.
2. Select the **Mail Format** tab.
3. Click the [ Signature Picker... ] button to open the Signature Picker dialog box.
4. From the list box, select the signature you want to edit.
5. Click the [ Edit... ] button to open the Edit Signature dialog box.
6. Make changes to the signature text, paragraph alignment (click [ Paragraph... ]), or font (click [ Font... ]) as needed. To redo the signature completely, click [ Clear ] and type a new signature.
7. Click the [ OK ] button to exit the Edit Signature dialog box.
8. Click the [ OK ] button to exit the Signature Picker dialog box.
9. Click the [ OK ] button to exit the Options dialog box.

### Delete a Signature

1. Choose **Tools, Options** to open the Options dialog box.
2. Select the **Mail Format** tab.
3. Click the `Signature Picker...` button to open the Signature Picker dialog box.
4. From the **Signature** list box, select the signature you want to remove.
5. Click the `Remove` button to delete the signature from the list box.
6. Click the `OK` button to exit the Signature Picker dialog box.
7. Click the `OK` button again to exit the Options dialog box.

*See Also* Email

## SPELL CHECK

You quickly can check your email messages for spelling errors before sending them. Outlook includes Microsoft's popular spell check tool.

### Run a Spell Check

1. After completing the email message in the message form window, move the cursor to the beginning of the message text.
2. Choose **Tools, Spelling**.
3. If the spell checker finds a misspelling, it highlights the word in the message text and opens the Spelling dialog box.

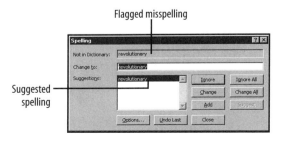

Flagged misspelling

Suggested spelling

**4.** Click the [ Change ] button to correct the word and use the spell checker's suggestion.

**5.** If the word is a name or proper noun, click the [ Ignore ] button to skip the word.

**6.** When the spell check is complete, click the [ OK ] button.

---

**TIP**

To permanently add a proper noun to the spell checker's dictionary, click the [ Add ] button from the Spelling dialog box.

---

# STATIONERY

If you prefer to give your email messages a more graphical look, consider using Outlook's stationery. The stationery feature lets you set a background color, specify a font, and add artwork to your email messages. This feature works only if you use HTML as your message format, instead of plain text (the default setting) or rich text format.

### Assign Stationery

**1.** Choose **Tools, Options** to display the Options dialog box.

**2.** Select the **Mail Format** tab.

**3.** Click the **Send in This Message Format** drop-down arrow and select **HTML**.

**4.** Click the [ Stationery Picker... ] button to open the Stationery Picker dialog box.

**5.** Scroll through the **Stationery** list box and select the stationery you want to use.

**6.** Click the [ OK ] button to close the Stationery Picker dialog box.

**7.** Click the [ OK ] button to close the Options dialog box.

**TIP**

When you first open a new message form after assigning stationery, a prompt box appears asking whether you want to use Word as your default email editor. Word is more adept at handling graphics that are typically a part of stationery. Click the [ No ] button to continue using Outlook or click the [ Yes ] button to use Word as your email editor.

### Customize Stationery

1. Choose **Tools, Options** to display the Options dialog box.

2. Select the **Mail Format** tab.

3. Click the [ Stationery Picker... ] button to open the Stationery Picker dialog box. (Be sure the **Send in This Message Format** box shows **HTML**, or you won't be able to open the Stationery Picker dialog box.)

4. Scroll through the **Stationery** list box and select the stationery you want to use.

5. Click the [ Edit... ] button to open the Edit Stationery dialog box.

6. Change the font, picture, text, or background color options as needed. Check the **Preview** area to see how the settings look.

7. When finished, click the [ OK ] button to close the Edit Stationery dialog box.

8. Click the [ OK ] button to close the Stationery Picker dialog box.

9. Click the [ OK ] button to close the Options dialog box.

### Turn Off Stationery for a Single Message

1. To turn off the stationery feature for a single email message, open the **Format** menu in the message form window and choose **Plain Text**.

2. Click the [ Yes ] button in the prompt box that appears.

### Turn Off Stationery for All Messages

1. Choose **Tools, Options** to display the Options dialog box.
2. Select the **Mail Format** tab.
3. Click the **Send in This Message Format** drop-down arrow and select **Plain Text**.
4. Click the [ OK ] button to close the Options dialog box.

> **TIP**
> To continue using the HTML format for your email messages, but not apply stationery, click the **Use This Stationery by Default** drop-down arrow on the Mail Format tab and choose **None**.

*See Also* Email

## TASKPAD
see Tasks    pg 124

## TASKS

Use Outlook's Tasks folder to keep track of things you need to do, such as steps for completing a project or arranging an event. Tasks can be as complex as a year-long project or as simple as a shopping list you need to fill on the way home. After you create a Task List, you can keep track of the tasks and check them off as you complete them. You can choose to view your Task List in the Tasks folder or in the Calendar folder.

### Add a New Task from the Tasks Folder

1. Click the **Tasks** icon on the Outlook bar to open the Tasks folder.
2. Choose **Actions, New Task**, click the New button on the Outlook toolbar, or press Ctrl+Shift+K on the keyboard.
3. The Task form window opens, and you can fill out information detailing the task. With the **Task** tab displayed, enter the subject or title of the task in the **Subject** text box.

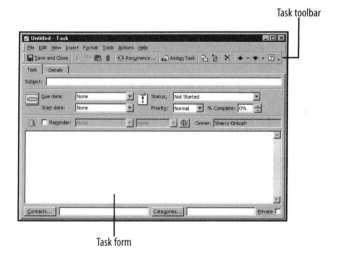

Task toolbar

Task form

4. If the task has a due date, click the **Due Date** drop-down arrow and choose a due date from the calendar or type in a date or time. (You also can enter a start date, if needed.)
5. Use the **Status** drop-down list to select a status setting for the project: **Not Started, In Progress, Completed, Waiting on Someone Else**, or **Deferred**. As you manage your Task List, you can update the status as needed.
6. Use the **Priority** drop-down list to give the task a priority level: **Normal, Low**, or **High**.

7. Use the **% Complete** box to specify a percentage of completeness, if needed.
8. To assign a reminder to the task, enable the **Reminder** check box and use the drop-down arrows to select when you want to be reminded.
9. Use the **Notes** box to enter any notes about the task.
10. After you finish filling out the Task form, click the ![Save and Close] button. The task is added to your Tasks folder's Task List.

> **TIP**
> To record statistics about a task, such as billable time, or mileage, display the **Details** tab of the Task form window and use the options there to record additional information.

**Add a Task Directly to the Tasks List**

1. Click the **Task** icon on the Outlook bar to open the Tasks folder.
2. Click the **Click Here to Add a New Task** line on the Task List.

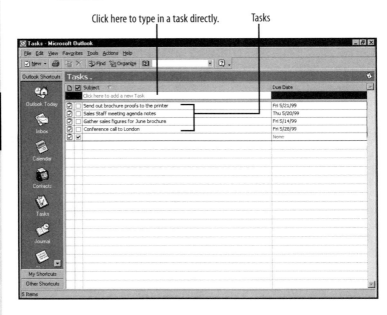

Click here to type in a task directly.    Tasks

**127**

3. Type the task description.

4. Click in the **Due Date** column and enter a due date, or use the drop-down arrow to assign a due date to the task.

5. Press ⏎Enter, and the task is added to the Task List.

### Add a New Task from the TaskPad

1. Click the **Calendar** 📅 icon on the Outlook bar to open the Calendar folder.

2. Click the **Click Here to Add a New Task** line on the TaskPad.

3. Type the task description.

4. Press ⏎Enter, and the task is added to the list.

### Edit a Task

1. Click the **Task** 📋 icon on the Outlook bar to open the Tasks folder.

2. To edit a task, double-click on the task in the Task List.

3. Make any changes to the task information as needed, such as a change in priority or completion.

4. Click the 💾 Save and Close icon on the Task toolbar to save your changes.

---

**TIP**

To edit a task from the TaskPad in the Calendar folder, double-click on the task in the TaskPad list to open the task.

---

### Delete a Task

1. Click the **Task** 📋 button on the Outlook bar to open the Tasks folder.

2. Select the task you want to remove, and click the **Delete** ✖ button on the Outlook toolbar. Or right-click on the task and choose **Delete**.

**S**
**T**
**U**

## Mark a Task As Completed

1. Click the **Task** [icon] icon on the Outlook bar to open the Tasks folder.

2. Enable the **Completed** check box (the second column in the Task List) for the task you want to mark.

3. A check mark appears in the box beside the task, and the task is displayed with a strikethrough line indicating that the task is complete.

---

**TIP**

You also can mark a task as complete in the Task form window. Open the Task form, click the **Status** drop-down arrow, and choose **Completed**. Or click the **Mark Complete** [icon] button on the Task form's toolbar.

---

## Send a Task Request

1. To assign an existing task to someone on your email list, open the Task form window for the task.

2. Click the [Assign Task] button on the Task form's toolbar.

3. Click inside the **To** text box and enter the person's email address (or click the To button and choose an address from your Address Book).

4. To keep the task listed in your Task List, enable the **Keep an Updated Copy of This Task on My Task List** check box.

5. To be informed when the task is completed, enable the **Send Me a Status Report When This Task Is Complete** check box.

6. Click the [Send] button to email the task request.

---

**TIP**

Another way to send a task request from the Tasks folder is to choose **Actions, New Task Request**. Or press Ctrl+⬆Shift+U.

---

***See Also*** Customize Outlook, Views

# TOOLBARS

The Outlook toolbar offers you shortcuts to the most common Outlook commands. By default, Outlook displays the Standard toolbar, but you also can display the Advanced toolbar, which includes buttons for navigating folders, and the Web toolbar, which has buttons for navigating Web pages. You can choose to hide or display these toolbars as needed. In addition, many of Outlook's forms include toolbars. You also can customize which buttons appear on the toolbars to suit your work needs.

### Display/Hide a Toolbar

1. Right-click on the toolbar and select the toolbar you want to display or hide. A check mark next to the toolbar name means it's already displayed.

2. You also can choose **View, Toolbars**, and select or deselect the toolbar you want to display or hide.

### View Hidden Buttons

1. Click the **More Buttons** ⊡ button at the far-right end of the toolbar to view additional buttons that might be available.

### Customize a Toolbar

1. Choose **Tools, Customize** to open the Customize dialog box.

2. Select the **Toolbars** tab, and select the toolbar you want to customize.

3. To remove a button from the toolbar, simply drag it off the toolbar (leave the Customize dialog box open onscreen).

4. To add a new button to the toolbar, select the **Commands** tab in the Customize dialog box and locate the category and command you want to add.
5. Drag the button from the **Commands** list onto the toolbar.
6. After you finish customizing the toolbar, click the Close button to exit the Customize dialog box.

> **TIP**
> You can always return your toolbar to its original settings. Open the Customize dialog box, select the toolbar on the **Toolbars** tab, and click the Reset... button.

*See Also* Customize Outlook

# UNDO

> *Quick Tips*
>
> | Feature | Keyboard Shortcut |
> |---------|-------------------|
> | Undo    | Ctrl+Z            |

Use the Undo command to immediately undo your last action, such as deleting an Outlook item from a folder. Unlike other Microsoft Office programs, the Undo command can undo only one action as opposed to multiple actions.

**Use the Undo Command**

1. Choose **Edit, Undo** or press Ctrl+Z.

*See Also* Redo

## URL
see Web Page    pg 135

## VCARDS

A vCard is a virtual business card users exchange on the Internet that contains pertinent contact information about a person. Outlook lets you save a contact as a vCard, or save vCards you receive in email messages and turn them into contacts.

### Save a Contact As a vCard

1. To turn any contact into a vCard, first open the Contacts folder; click the **Contacts** 📇 icon on the Outlook Bar.

2. Double-click on the contact you want to save as a vCard.

3. Open the Contact form's **File** menu and choose **Export to vCard File**.

4. If needed, select a folder to save the vCard to, and then click the [💾 Save] button to confirm.

5. Click the Contact form's **Close** [✕] button to exit the form.

### Import a vCard

1. Choose **File, Import and Export**.

2. Select **Import a vCard File** from the list box.

3. Open the Contact form's **File** menu and choose **Export to vCard File**.

4. Click the [Next >] button to continue.

5. Locate the vCard file you want to import; then double-click on the filename.

---

**TIP**

To quickly import a vCard you received in an email message, double-click on the vCard attachment, fill in any additional contact information, and then click the [💾 Save and Close] button.

---

V
W
X

## Send a vCard in an Email Message

1. Click the **Contact** 🔲 icon on the Outlook Bar to open the Contacts folder.

2. Select the contact you want to send as a vCard.

3. Choose **Actions, Forward As vCard**.

4. A Message form opens with the contact's vCard attached. Finish addressing and filling out the message; then click the ⬛ Send ▾ button to send the message to the Outbox.

## Save a vCard Received in an Email Message

1. Open the message containing the vCard attachment.

2. Right-click over the attachment and select **Save As**.

3. Select a folder to save the vCard to; then click the 🔲 Save button to save the file.

---

**TIP**

To quickly view a vCard attachment, double-click on the attachment in the email message.

---

## Include a vCard with Your Signature

1. Open the **Tools** menu and choose **Options** to display the Options dialog box.

2. Click the **Mail Format** tab.

3. Click the Signature Picker... button to open the Signature Picker dialog box.

4. Click the New... button to open the Create New Signature dialog box.

5. Type a name for the signature and select any options, and then click Next > to continue.

6. Fill in the signature text and format as needed. To assign an existing vCard to the signature, click the **Attach This Business Card (vCard) to This Signature** drop-down arrow and select the vCard.

7. To create a new vCard, click the New vCard from Contact... button.

**133**

8. Select the person you want to create a vCard for and click the [ Add -> ] button.

9. Click the [ OK ] button when finished.

10. Click the [ Finish ] button to finish creating a signature.

11. Click [ OK ] to close the Signature Picker dialog box.

12. To use the signature with the vCard you just created, be sure it's displayed in the **Use this Signature by Default** list box in the Options dialog box (if it's not, click the drop-down arrow and select it from the list).

13. Click [ OK ] to close the Options dialog box.

*See Also* Contacts, Email, File Attachment, Signature

# VIEWS

Each Outlook folder offers you several ways to view information. The Calendar lets you view your schedule by day, week, workweek, or month by clicking associated buttons on the Outlook toolbar, for example. You also can view specific portions of information by using the Current View command from any Outlook folder. You can create a custom view that shows only the information you designate.

### Change the Current View

1. Choose **View, Current View**.

2. Depending on the folder you're using, select an option for viewing the information, such as **By Category**.

### Create a Custom View

1. Choose **View, Current View, Define Views**.

2. Click the [ New... ] button to open the Create a New View dialog box.

3. Enter a name for the view you're creating in the **Name of New View** text box.

4. In the **Type of View** list box, select a view type.

V
W
X

5. Use the **Can Be Used On** options to designate where the view can be used.

6. Click the [ OK ] button to close the Create a New View dialog box and open the View Settings dialog box.

7. Use the various buttons to change which items are displayed in the view. Each button lets you change different features, such as fonts or fields.

8. When you're finished, click the [ OK ] button to close the View Settings dialog box.

9. To use the new view, which is selected by default, click the [ Apply View ] button. To exit without applying the new view, click the [ Close ] button.

10. To apply the new view at any time, choose **View, Current View**. Then select the name of the view from the submenu.

---

**TIP**

You can customize any existing Outlook view. Display the view you want to customize and choose **View, Current View, Customize Current View**. Use the various buttons in the View Summary dialog box to change fonts, fields, and other display settings.

---

### Edit a Custom View

1. Choose **View, Current View, Define Views** to open the Define Views dialog box.

2. Select the view you want to edit and click the [ Modify... ] button.

3. Use the various buttons to change view fields, fonts, and other settings.

4. Click the [ OK ] button when finished making changes to close the View Settings dialog box.

5. Click the [ Close ] button to close the Define Views dialog box, or click the [ Apply View ] button to apply the modified view right away.

> **TIP**
>
> To rename a view rather than modify it, choose the view, click the ⟨Rename...⟩ button, and give the view a new name.

### Delete a Custom View

1. Choose **View, Current View, Define Views**.
2. Select the view you want to delete and click the ⟨Delete⟩ button.
3. Click the ⟨OK⟩ button to confirm the deletion.
4. Click the ⟨Close⟩ button to exit the dialog box.

# WEB PAGE

You can view Web pages from within Outlook, accessing them through the Favorites menu. You also can use Outlook's Web toolbar to navigate Web pages and Web sites, including typing in URLs (*Uniform Resource Locators,* also called *Web addresses*). In addition, any links you click on in email messages will open the Internet Explorer browser window and you can view Web pages from there. You must log onto your Internet account in order to use Outlook's Web features.

### Display the Web Toolbar

1. Choose **View, Toolbars, Web**.

   or

1. Right-click the Standard toolbar or menu bar and choose **Web** from the pop-up menu.

> **TIP**
>
> The Web toolbar appears whenever you select a Web page from the Favorites menu. To hide the toolbar, right-click a blank area of the toolbar and choose **Web**.

**Enter a URL**

1. Click inside the **Address** text box on the Web toolbar and enter the URL you want to view. If viewing files on your computer, enter the path to the file you want to view instead.
2. Press ⏎**Enter**, and the page or file appears in the folder display area of the Outlook window.

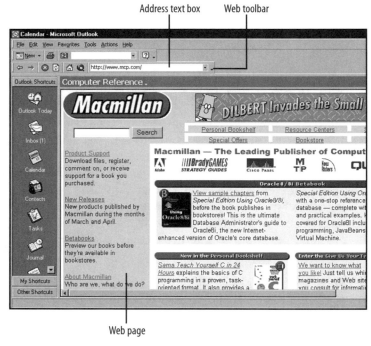

**Navigate the Web**

1. Click the **Back** button to return to a previous Web page you've viewed.
2. Click the **Forward** button to return to the page you were viewing before you clicked the **Back** button.
3. Click the **Stop Current Jump** button to stop the current page from loading onscreen.
4. Click the **Refresh Current Page** button to reload the current page.

**5.** Click the **Start Page** 🏠 button to view the default home or start page for your default browser.

**6.** Click the **Search the Web** 🔍 button to conduct a Web search.

### Add a Web Page Shortcut to the Outlook Bar

**1.** Display the Web page in Outlook.

**2.** Choose **File, New, Outlook Bar Shortcut to Web Page**.

---

**TIP**

Another way to quickly add a shortcut to a Web page and place it on the Outlook Bar is to open the page, and then right-click on the Outlook Bar and choose **Outlook Bar Shortcut to Web Page**.

---

### Send a Web Page in an Email Message

**1.** Display the Web page in Outlook.

**2.** Choose **Actions, Send Web Page by E-Mail**.

**3.** Enter the email address of the person you want to send the page to, fill out the message form, and send it.

### Save the Calendar As a Web Page

**1.** Open the Calendar folder; click the **Calendar** 📅 button on the Outlook Bar.

**2.** Choose **File, Save As Web Page**.

**3.** Specify which dates to display on the page.

**4.** If you want to include the appointment details, leave the **Include Appointment Details** check box selected. If not, deselect the option.

**5.** To include a background with the page, enable the **Use Background Graphic** check box and use the [ Browse... ] button to locate the graphic file or background you want to use.

**6.** Give the page a name by entering a title in the **Calendar Title** text box.

7. Click inside the **File Name** text box and enter a name for the Web page file you're creating. Use the Browse... button to choose a specific folder to save to.

8. Click the Save button. Outlook saves your page and opens it in your default browser.

*See Also* Calendar, Email, Favorites, Outlook Bar

# WORD

If you have Microsoft Word, you might prefer to use it as your email editor instead of Outlook. Using Word lets you tap into features, such as AutoCorrect, tables, and themes, that are not available in Outlook.

### Turn Word On or Off As Your Email Editor

1. Choose **Tools, Options** to open the Options dialog box.

2. Click the **Mail Format** tab.

3. Select or deselect the **Use Microsoft Word to Edit E-Mail Messages** check box to turn the feature on or off.

4. Click the OK button to exit the Options dialog box.

---

**TIP**

To use Word as your email editor for a single message, open the Inbox folder (press **Ctrl+Shift+I**); then choose **Actions, New Mail Message Using, Microsoft Word**.

---

*See Also* Email

# WORK OFFLINE

You're working online when you're connected to your Internet account and emailing messages as you write them. You may prefer to work offline to compose email messages, and then go online at a later time to send them all at once.

You can switch between online and offline modes in Outlook. (This feature isn't available if you're using Outlook in Corporate/Workgroup mode.)

### Switch to Offline Mode

1. To work offline, choose **File, Work Offline**.
2. You now can compose messages and click the [Send] button, but the messages aren't actually sent until you log onto your Internet account and click the [Send/Receive] button on the Outlook toolbar.

*See Also* Accounts

## YEARLY EVENTS/OCCURRENCES

see Event    pg 49

# APPENDIX A

## GETTING STARTED WITH OUTLOOK

If you're absolutely new to Outlook, this appendix offers an overview on using the program and navigating the program window. If you're new to computers in general, you might try a book about Windows basics, such as *The Complete Idiot's Guide to Windows 98*, published by Que.

### What Can I Do with Outlook?

Outlook is all about managing personal information, whether it's in the form of appointments, email, or a simple To Do list. Outlook acts as your own personal secretary and never takes a vacation. Use Outlook 2000 to

- Help you remember important appointments
- Keep track of phone calls you make
- Organize the names and addresses of people you contact the most
- Send and receive email messages
- Itemize important tasks you need to complete
- Jot down notes
- Decide which email messages to save or delete
- Remind you of events, such as anniversaries
- View Web pages
- Manage computer files and folders

Those are just a few of the things you can do with Outlook. The more you use the program, the more things you'll come up with yourself. You'll quickly find that Outlook is well suited for use at work or at home, wherever you need to manage personal information.

# Appendix

## What's Onscreen?

When you first open Outlook, the program window displays the typical window elements found in other Microsoft-based programs. Take a look at the following figure to identify each major component of the Outlook window.

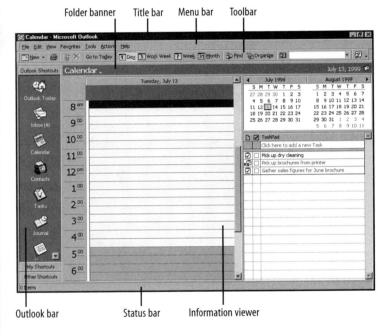

Here's a rundown of each onscreen item:

**Title bar** Lists the name of the program along with which feature folder is open, such as the Inbox or Calendar. You'll find the program window controls (**Minimize, Maximize/Restore, Close**) at the far-right end of the Title bar.

**Menu bar** Lists each menu category, which in turn lists commands for activating features and performing tasks. To view a menu, click the menu name. To select a command from a menu, simply click the command.

# Appendix 143

**Toolbar**   Lists icon buttons you can click to quickly activate a command or feature. To learn what a particular button does, hover your mouse pointer over the button to reveal a screentip with the button's name.

**Outlook Bar**   Lists icons for each of Outlook's main features and group buttons. To open a feature folder, click its corresponding icon on the Outlook Bar. To change which group of icons is displayed, click a group button: Outlook Shortcuts, My Shortcuts, or Other Shortcuts.

**Folder banner**   Outlook's main features (also called *modules*) are organized into folders. When you open a feature, the Information Viewer displays the feature along with a folder banner at the top identifying the feature.

**Information Viewer**   The large area onscreen for viewing the feature you're working with.

**Status bar**   Displays onscreen status regarding the feature you're currently working with, such as number of email messages in the Inbox or the total number of contacts in the Contacts folder.

## How Is Outlook Organized?

Outlook has seven main features—or modules—to help you manage information, and each is organized as a folder. You'll find all seven of these features listed as shortcut icons on the Outlook Bar on the far-left side of the program window. You can also access them through the Folder List. Here's a description of each of the main folders:

**Inbox**   Keeps track of email messages you receive.

**Calendar**   Use to maintain your schedule, noting appointments and events.

**Contacts**   A database collection of names, addresses, phone numbers, and email addresses of people you contact.

**Tasks**   Track important things you need to do, whether it's as simple as a grocery list or a complex list of tasks you need to track for a work project.

**Journal**   Use this feature to keep a record of phone calls you make, documents you open, or activities you perform that require you to note the day, time, and minutes spent on the task.

**Notes**   Use this feature to quickly write out electronic notes when you don't want to open your word processor or write something down on paper.

**Deleted Items**   Every Outlook item you delete is thrown into this folder where it awaits permanent removal from your computer.

---

**WHAT ABOUT THE OUTLOOK TODAY ICON?**

This feature grabs information from all the Outlook folders and places it in one spot for a quick glance at the day's priorities, such as appointments, due dates, and so on. From here, you can check out things you need to do and link back to the original item it's associated with.

---

Outlook's many folders are organized into groups. In addition to the main folders previously described, Outlook has other folder shortcuts you can access through the Outlook Bar. The following figure shows the Outlook Bar elements. Use the arrow buttons to view different portions of the Outlook Bar or use the group buttons to view different sets of shortcut icons.

# Appendix

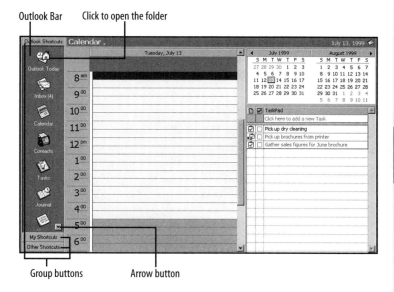

The **Outlook Shortcuts** group contains shortcut icons to the seven features previously described. Here's a description of the shortcut icons found in the **My Shortcuts** group:

**Drafts** Stores unfinished email messages you're composing.

**Outbox** Holds email messages waiting to be sent the next time you log on to your Internet account or network server.

**Sent Items** Keeps a copy of every email message you send.

Here's a description of the shortcut icons found in **Other Shortcuts** group:

**My Computer** View the drives and folders on your computer.

**My Documents** This folder stores the files you work with the most, such as document or spreadsheet files.

**Favorites** Holds your favorite files and Web pages.

# Appendix

> **CAN I CUSTOMIZE SHORTCUT ICONS?**
>
> You can customize Outlook to suit your own needs, which means you may add, remove, rename, or move shortcut icons around. Turn to the topic **Outlook Bar** to learn more about customizing the icons.

Another way to view Outlook's folders, including any subfolders within a main feature folder, is to use the Folder List. To display the list, choose **View, Folder List** or click the drop-down arrow on the Folder banner. The next figure shows an example of what the Folder List looks like when displayed onscreen.

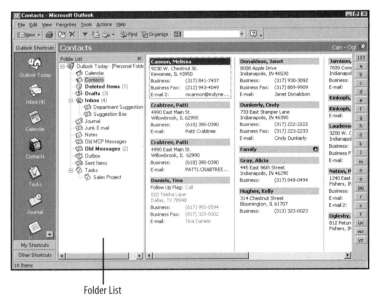

Folder List

Like the Window's My Computer or Windows Explorer features, the Folder List shows the Outlook folder hierarchy and where each Outlook item is stored. You can easily create new folders to help you organize items.

# Appendix

**147**

> **CAN I MANAGE MY COMPUTER FILES FROM OUTLOOK?**
>
> Yes, that's one of the many features Outlook offers. To learn more about working with computer files from within Outlook, see the topic **File Management**.

## Program Basics

To move around the Outlook program window, use the mouse to click various onscreen items. Depending on the folder you're using, you might also see scrollbars you can use to view different portions of the screen. Click the scrollbar arrows to change the view.

To issue commands in Outlook, use the Menu bar, Toolbar buttons, or keyboard shortcuts. Depending on the command you activate, a dialog box might appear. Dialog boxes offer additional options and choices you can make before actually issuing a command. For example, if you want to print an Outlook item with the **File**, **Print** command, a Print dialog box opens (see the next figure) and you can choose how many copies to print, which printer to use, and other printing options.

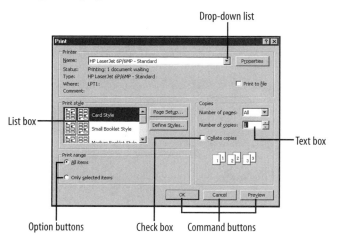

If you prefer using the keyboard to issue commands, you can open menus by pressing the Alt key followed by the underlined letter of the menu you want to view. For example, to display the **File** menu, press **Alt+F**. To activate a command from the menu, simply press the corresponding underlined letter of the command.

### How to Fill Out Outlook Forms

When creating new items in Outlook, such as an appointment or a contact, use a form. Outlook's forms resemble paper forms you use to fill out information. For example, the Contact form shown in the next figure has text boxes (called *fields*) where you can enter the person's name, address, and phone number. The form acts just like a window: You can minimize, maximize, move it, or resize it as you like.

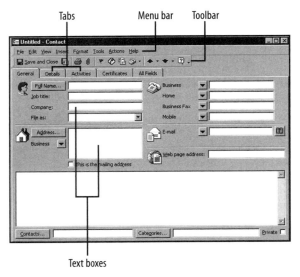

# Appendix 149

Many of the forms have their own Menu bar and Toolbar with commands related specifically to the type of item you're creating. To hold all the possible types of entry fields, the form information fields are organized into tabs, similar to a paper file folder. To view a tab, click on the tab name.

To fill out a form, click inside the field where you want to enter text. Press the **Tab** button on the keyboard to move from field to field, or just click inside the next field. If you make a mistake while typing, use the **Backspace** and **Delete** keys to fix errors. After you save and close the form, you can always reopen it again and edit the information.

That wraps up our overview of how Outlook looks and how it works. You're now ready to plunge in and start using the program yourself. Just flip through the reference guide for help with new topics you want to tackle. Good luck!

# INDEX

### A

accounts (Internet)
  changing default, 3
  properties, 2-4
  removing, 2-4
  setting up, 1-3
  viewing, 1-3

Accounts command (Tools menu), 1

actions
  redoing, 109
  undoing, 130

Actions menu commands
  Flag for Follow Up, 111
  Forward As vCard, 132
  New All Day Event, 49
  New Distribution List, 101
  New Mail Using, 138
  New Meeting Request to Contact, 82
  New Task, 125
  New Task Request, 128
  Plan a Meeting, 80
  Send Web Page by E-Mail, 137

Actual Size button, 106

Add Entries to Subscriber Database dialog box, 86

Add New Group command (Outlook Bar menu), 96

Add New Member dialog box, 102

Add to Favorites command (Favorites menu), 51

Add to Junk Senders List command (Junk E-Mail menu), 48

adding
  Favorites, 51
  groups (Outlook Bar), 96

notes (Notes folder), 89
notes on members (personal distribution list), 102
shortcuts (groups), 97
tasks, 126-127
Web page shortcuts to Outlook bar, 137
words to dictionary, 122

adding to personal distribution list, 102

Address Book, 4, 26. *See also* contacts
  addresses
    *adding, 5-6*
    *deleting, 6-7*
    *editing, 6*
    *finding, 7-8*
  exporting, 9
  groups, 7-9
  importing, 8-9

addresses, 26. *See also* contacts
  adding, 5-7
  deleting, 6-7
  editing, 6
  finding, 7-8

Advanced Find, 55-56

Advanced Find dialog box, 55-56

Advanced Options dialog box, 110-112

Advanced tab, 56

alarm (reminders), changing sound, 112

All Attendees list, 80

All Day Event check box, 49

Alt key (opening menu commands), 78

Answer Wizard, 68

Appointment form, 10

Appointment Recurrence dialog box, 50

appointments, 113. *See also* reminders
  categories, assigning, 13
  copying tasks into, 30
  deleting, 13
  editing, 13
  moving, 13
  printing, 14
  reminders, 12, 111
  setting, 10-11
  "show time as" setting, 12

Archive command (File menu), 16

archives
  AutoArchive
    *folders, 15*
    *setting up, 14-15*
  manual, 16

archiving items, 72

assigning
  categories, 22, 25
  permission status to Net Folders, 86
  reminders
    *appointments, 111*
    *contacts, 111-112*
    *tasks, 111*

attaching
  files to email messages, 52-53
  vCards (signatures), 132-133

attachments
  files, 52
    *opening, 53*
    *saving, 53*
  saving, 117
  viewing (QuickView), 109

Attendee Availability tab, 82

AutoArchive
  folders, 15
  Journal entries, 77
  setting up, 14-15

AutoDialer, 16-17

automatic Journal entries, 75-76

autopicking meeting times, 82

AutoPreview, 18-19, 42

AutoPreview command (View menu), 42

## B-C

Back button, 136

Bcc Field command (View menu), 46

Bcc text box, 46

blind carbon copies, 46

blind carbon copying email messages, 46

Browse dialog box, 91

buttons, 129. *See also individual button names*

By Category view, 22

Calendar, 19, 113. *See also* reminders
  customizing features, 35-36
  displaying dates, 20
  Go To command, 63
  panes, sizing, 20
  saving as Web page, 137
  views, changing, 19-20

Calendar button, 50, 137

calendar days (Outlook Today page), setting, 99

calendar events, 49-50

Calendar folder, 11, 50, 124, 137

Calendar icon, 49

Calendar Options, 35

Calendar Options dialog box, 35, 79

Calendar Title text box, 137

calling contacts
  AutoDialer, 16-17
  speed dialing, 17-18

carbon copies, 45-46

carbon copying email messages, 45-46

categories, 21
adding, 22-23
assigning, 22, 25
deleting, 23
organizing items into, 92-93
viewing, 22

Categories command (Edit menu), 23

Categories dialog box, 22

Cc text box, 45

Change Your View list, 93

changing
alarm sound (reminders), 112
color (notes), 89-90
default settings (reminders), 110
encoding language (email messages), 62
format (email messages), 62
page setup options (Print Preview), 106-107
printer, 104
properties (printer), 108
size (shortcut icons), 97
views, 88, 133

check boxes
All Day Event, 49
Collate Copies, 105
Completed, 57, 128
Default Reminder, 110
Include Appointment Details, 137
Keep an Updated Copy of This Task on My Task List, 128
Microsoft Word to edit email messages, 138
Publish My Free/Busy Information, 80
Reminder, 111, 126
Request a Read Receipt for This Message, 48
Save Copies of Messages in Sent Items Folder, 118
Send Me a Status Report When This Task Is Complete, 128
Standard and Formatting Toolbars Share One Row, 47

This Is an Online Meeting Using, 82
Use Background Graphic, 137
When Starting, Go Directly to Outlook Today, 98

Check Names button, 45

checking
email, 41
spelling, 121-122

Click Here link, 94

Close button, 109

closing Organize pane, 92

Collate Copies check box, 105

color
notes, changing, 38, 89-90
organizing messages with, 93

color coding junk email messages, 94

columns, customizing, 70-71

commands
Actions menu
*Flag for Follow Up, 111*
*Forward As vCard, 132*
*New All Day Event, 49*
*New Distribution List, 101*
*New Mail Using, 138*
*New Meeting Request to Contact, 82*
*New Task, 125*
*New Task Request, 128*
*Plan a Meeting, 80*
*Send Web Page by E-Mail, 137*
Current View menu
*Customize Current View, 134*
*Define Views, 133-135*
Edit menu
*Categories, 23*
*Copy, 28, 100*
*Cut, 84, 100*
*Paste, 84, 100*
*Redo, 110*
*Undo, 130*

## B-C

## 153

File menu
  Archive, 16
  Exit, 51
  Export to vCard file, 131
  Folder, 58
  Import and Export, 8, 131
  New, 101, 137
  New Folder, 85
  Open File for Editing, 109
  Page Setup, 107-108
  Print, 104
  Save As, 117
  Save As Web Page, 137
  Share, 86
  Work Offline, 139
Folder menu (New Folder), 58
Format menu
  HTML, 62
  Plain Text, 62, 123
  Rich Text, 62
Forms menu (Design a
  Form), 61
Help menu (Hide the Office
  Assistant), 65
Insert menu (Signature), 119
Junk E-Mail menu (Add to
  Junk Senders List), 48
message context menu (Junk
  E-Mail), 48
New Mail Using menu
  (Microsoft Word), 138
New menu
  Distribution List, 101
  Post in This Folder, 87
Outlook Bar menu
  Add New Group, 96
  Outlook Bar Shortcuts, 97
  Remove Group, 96
  Rename Group, 96
Page Setup menu (Define Print
  Styles), 108
Programs menu (Microsoft
  Outlook), 90
Settings menu (Taskbar &
  Start), 91
Share menu (This Folder), 86
Start menu (Settings), 91
Toolbars menu (Web), 135

Tools menu
  Accounts, 1
  Customize, 31, 47, 129
  Forms, 61
  Map Network Drive, 54
  Options, 14, 62, 79, 103,
    110-112, 118-119,
    132, 138
  Rules Wizard, 114
  Send/Receive, 41
  Services, 3
  Spelling, 121
View menu
  Bcc, 46
  Current View, 133-134
  Folder List, 59-60
  Go To, 63
  HTML, 46
  Preview Pane, 42, 103
  Rich Text, 46
  Toolbars, 129, 135

Commands tab, 130

Commands list, 130

Completed check box, 57, 128

contacts, 24-26, 113, 131. See also
  Address Book; addresses;
  reminders; vCards
    adding, 24-25
    AutoDialing, 16-17
    categories, assigning, 25
    copying, 29-30
    creating email messages
      from, 47
    customizing features, 36-37
    deleting, 26
    editing, 26
    exporting, 27-28
    finding, 26
    flagging for follow up, 57
    importing, 27
    printing, 26
    reminders, assigning
      to, 111-112
    saving as vCards, 131
    speed dialing, 17-18
    view, changing, 25

Contacts folder, 47, 131

Contacts form, 131

Contacts icon, 131

contents (help), looking up topics, 67-68

Copy command (Edit menu), 28, 100

copying
contacts, 29-30
items, 28-29, 72
tasks into appointments, 30
text (forms), 29

Corporate/Workgroup mode, 1
accounts
*properties, 3-4*
*removing, 4*
*setting up, 3*
changing to Internet Only mode, 4
mail services options, 34
services, viewing, 3

Create New Folder dialog box, 58

Create New Signature dialog box, 35, 119, 132

Create New View dialog box, 133

Create Shortcut dialog box, 91

creating
email messages (contacts), 47
folders, 58-59
Net Folders, 85-86
personal distribution list, 101
signatures, 119
subscriber list (Net Folders), 86

Current View command (View menu), 133-134

Current View menu commands
Customize Current View, 134
Define Views, 133-135

custom views, deleting, 135

Customize command (Tools menu), 31, 47, 129

Customize Current View command (Current View menu), 134

Customize dialog box, 31, 129

Customize Outlook Today button, 98

customizing
Outlook, 30
*Calendar features, 35-36*
*contacts features, 36-37*
*email features, 33*
*email signatures, 35*
*Inbox columns, 70-71*
*journal features, 37*
*large icons, 31*
*mail delivery options, 34*
*mail format options, 34*
*mail services options, 34*
*menu commands, 31-32*
*notes features, 38*
*Office Assistant, 65*
*personalized menus, 31*
*Startup folder, 38*
*tasks features, 36*
*toolbar, 32-33*
pages (Outlook Today), 99
panes (Preview), 103-104
stationery, 123
toolbars, 129-130
views, 133-134

Cut command (Edit menu), 84, 100

## D

Date Navigator (Calendar), 20

default format (email messages), setting, 62

default pages (Outlook Today), setting, 98

Default Reminder check box, 110

default settings
print styles, 108
reminders, changing, 110
toolbars, resetting, 130

Define Print Styles command (Page Setup menu), 108

Define Print Styles dialog box, 108

Define Views command (Current View menu), 133-135

# 155

# INDEX

Define Views dialog box, 134

Delete button, 44, 90, 127

Deleted Items folder, 39

deleting
addresses, 6-7
appointments, 13
categories, 23
contacts, 26
custom views, 135
email messages, 44
events, 50
folders, 59
groups (Outlook Bar), 96
items, 72
Journal entries, 76
notes, 90
rules, 115
shortcuts (groups), 97
signatures, 121
tasks, 127

Delivery Options settings, 48

Design a Form command (Forms menu), 61

Design Form dialog box, 61

designing forms, 61

Details tab, 126

Device Options tab, 108

dialog boxes
Add Entries to Subscriber, 86
Add New Member, 102
Advanced Find, 55-56
Advanced Options, 112
Appointment Recurrence, 50
Browse, 91
Calendar Options, 79
Categories, 22
Create New Folder, 58
Create New Signature, 35, 119, 132
Create New View, 133
Create Shortcut, 91
Customize, 31, 129
Define Print Styles, 108
Define Views, 134
Design Form, 61
Distribution List, 102

E-Mail Options, 118
Edit Signature, 119-120
Edit Stationery, 123
Find People, 8
Flag for Follow Up, 56
Free/Busy Options, 80
Import Rules From, 116
Insert File, 52
Internet Accounts, 1
Journal Options, 37
New Call, 16
Note Options, 90
Options, 14, 79, 103, 110, 116-119, 132, 138
Page Setup, 107-108
Plan a Meeting, 80
Preview Pane, 103
Print, 104, 108
Properties, 15, 87, 108
Reminder Options, 111-112
Rules Wizard, 114
Save As, 117
Save Exported Rules As, 116
Select Attendees and Resources, 81
Select Folder, 99
Select Group Members, 7
Select Members, 101
Services, 3
Signatures Picker, 119, 133
Spelling, 122
Stationery Picker, 122
Taskbar Properties, 91
View Settings, 134
View Summary, 134

dictionary, adding words to, 122

dismissing reminders, 112

displaying
dates (Calendar), 20
dialog boxes (Options), 132
toolbars, 47, 129, 135

Distribution List command (New menu), 101

Distribution List dialog box, 102

drafting email messages, 47

drafts, opening, 47

**INDEX**

**D**

**156**

Drafts folder, 118

drag and drop, 29, 85

dragging
notes, 89
shortcuts (groups), 97

drop-down lists
Priority, 125
Status, 125, 128

**E**

E-Mail Options, 33

E-Mail Options dialog box, 33, 118

Edit menu commands
Categories, 23
Copy, 28, 100
Cut, 84, 100
Paste, 84, 100
Redo, 110
Undo, 130

Edit Signature dialog box, 119-120

Edit Stationery dialog box, 123

editing
addresses, 6
appointments, 13
contacts, 26
events, 50
Journal entries, 76
notes, 89
print styles, 108
rules, 115
signatures, 120
tasks, 127

email, 40. *See also* file attachments;
stationery
addresses
adding to Address Book, 5
default, setting, 6
AutoPreview, 18-19
checking, 41
customizing features, 33
Internet accounts
changing default, 3
properties, 2-4
removing, 2-4

setting up, 1-3
viewing, 1-3
mail delivery options, 34
mail format options, 34
mail services options, 34
messages
blind carbon copying, 46
carbon copying, 45-46
copying contacts into, 30
creating (Contacts), 47
deleting, 44
Delivery Options settings, 48
drafting, 47
encoding language,
changing, 62
files, attaching, 52-53
filtering, 94
flagging for follow up, 56-57
format, 62
formatting, 46
forwarding, 44, 62
HTML format, 124
junk, 94
marking as read/
unread, 44, 79
navigating, 43
organizing, 93
Outlook Today page (setting
to appear), 99
previewing, 42
priority, setting, 47-48
reading, 43
replying to, 43-44
sending (Outbox), 44, 95
sensitivity, setting, 47-48
sent, saving, 118
Tracking Options settings, 48
unfinished, saving, 118
vCards, sending as, 132
writing, 45
rules, 113
signatures, 35
creating, 119
deleting, 121
editing, 120
inserting, 119-120
sorting, 70
Web pages, sending as, 137

email editors (Word), 138

encoding language (email messages), changing, 62

end time
    events, setting, 49
    meetings, setting, 81

entering
    links, 78
    URLs, 136

entries (Journal)
    AutoArchiving, 77
    automatic, 75-76
    deleting, 76
    editing, 76
    finding, 77
    manual, 74-75
    printing, 76
    views, changing, 76

Event toolbar, 50

events, 49. *See also* appointments; calendar; reminders
    deleting, 50
    editing, 50
    recurring, setting, 50
    scheduling, 49-50
    start/end time, setting, 49

Exit command (File menu), 51

exiting
    Contacts form, 131
    Outlook, 51

Export to vCard file command (File menu), 131

exporting, 51
    Address Books, 9
    contacts, 27-28
    rules, 116

# F

Favorites, 51-52

Favorites folder, 51-52

Favorites icon, 59

Favorites list, 52

Favorites menu, 51-52, 135

Favorites menu commands (Add to Favorites), 51

Favorites shortcuts, 59

file attachments, 52
    opening, 53
    saving, 53, 117

File menu commands
    Archive, 16
    Exit, 51
    Export to vCard file, 131
    Folder, 58
    Import and Export, 8, 131
    New, 101, 137
    New Folder, 85
    Open File for Editing, 109
    Page Setup, 107-108
    Print, 104
    Print Preview, 105
    Save As, 117
    Save As Web Page, 137
    Share, 86
    Work Offline, 139

File Name text box, 52, 117, 138

files
    attaching (email messages), 52-53
    managing, 53
    My Computer, 59
    My Documents, 59
    opening, 54
    Outlook.exe, 91
    previewing, 109
    viewing, 53-54, 59

filtering (email messages), 94

Find feature (Advanced), 55-56

Find People dialog box, 8

Find tool, 54

finding
    addresses, 7-8
    contacts, 26
    items, 54-55
    Journal entries, 77

Flag for Follow Up, 56

Flag for Follow Up command (Actions menu), 111

Flag for Follow Up dialog box, 56

Flag for Follow Up icon, 56

flagged items, marking as complete, 57

flagging
contacts for follow up, 57
email messages for follow up, 56-57

flags, removing, 57. *See also* reminders

Folder command (File menu), 58

Folder List, 60

Folder List command (View menu), 59-60

Folder menu commands (New Folder), 58

folders
archiving, 15-16
Calendar, 50, 124, 137
Contacts, 47, 131
creating, 58-59
Deleted Items, 39
deleting, 59
Drafts, 118
Favorites, 51-52
managing, 58
My Computer, 59
My Documents, 54, 59
naming, 58
Net, 85
*creating, 85-86*
*posting to, 87*
*publishing, 86-87*
*subscriber list, creating, 86*
*updating, 87*
Notes, 88-89
organizing items into, 92
Outbox, 95
renaming, 59
Sent Items, 118
StartUp, 91
Startup, changing, 38
Tasks, 124
viewing, 59

following links, 78

fonts (notes), changing, 38

Fonts tab, 108

Format menu commands
HTML, 62
Plain Text, 62, 123
Rich Text, 62

Format tab, 106

formats
email messages, 62
HTML, 46
Plain Text, 46
Rich Text, 46

formatting email messages, 46

Formatting toolbar, 46-47

forms, 61
Contacts, *131*
designing, 61
Meeting, 81
text, copying, 29

Forms command (Tools menu), 61

Forms menu commands (Design a Form), 61

Forward As vCard command (Actions menu), 132

Forward button, 136

forwarding email messages, 44, 62

Free/Busy Options dialog box, 80

free/busy times, publishing, 79-80

## G-H

Go To command (View menu), 63

group buttons, 95

groups
adding, 96
deleting, 96
renaming, 96
shortcuts, 97

groups (Address Book), 7

Header/Footer tab, 107

**159**

help, 64
  Answer Wizard, 68
  contents, looking up
    topics, 67-68
  Help window, navigating, 67
  index, 68
  Internet, 68-69
  Office Assistant, 64-66
  printing topics, 68
  What's This?, 69

Help menu commands (Hide the
  Office Assistant), 65

Help window, navigating, 67

Hide the Office Assistant
  command (Help menu), 65

hiding
  Office Assistant, 65
  Outlook Bar, 95
  toolbars, 129, 135

HTML command
  Format menu, 62
  View menu, 46

HTML format, 46, 124

hyperlinks, 78. *See also* links

---

**I**

icons
  Calendar, 49
  Contacts, 131
  Favorites, 59
  Flag for Follow Up, 56
  large, 31
  Microsoft Outlook, 90
  Notes, 88
  Other Shortcut, 59
  shortcut, changing size, 97

Import and Export command (File
  menu), 8, 131

Import and Export Wizard, 8

Import Rules From dialog box, 116

importing
  Address Books, 8-9
  contacts, 27
  rules, 116
  vCards, 131

Inbox, 69
  columns, customizing, 70-71
  sorting messages, 70
  view, changing, 70

Inbox button, 41-42, 114

Inbox list, 43

Include Appointment Details
  check box, 137

index (help), 68

Insert File button, 52

Insert File dialog box, 52

Insert menu commands
  (Signature), 119

inserting signatures, 119-120

Internet (help), 68-69

Internet accounts
  changing default, 3
  properties, 2-4
  removing, 2-4
  setting up, 1-3
  viewing, 1-3

Internet Accounts dialog box, 1

Internet Only mode, 1
  accounts
    *changing default, 3*
    *properties, 2*
    *removing, 2*
    *setting up, 1*
    *viewing, 1*
  changing to, 4
  mail delivery options, 34

inviting to meetings, 81

items, 71
  archiving, 72
  copying, 72
  deleting, 72
  finding, 54-55
  flagged, marking as
    complete, 57
  moving, 72, 84-85
  opening, 71
  organizing
    *categories, 92-93*
    *folders, 92*
    *views, 93*

**160**

pasting, 84, 100
saving, 117
selecting, 71

## J

Journal, 73
customizing features, 37
entries
*AutoArchiving, 77*
*automatic, 75-76*
*deleting, 76*
*editing, 76*
*finding, 77*
*manual, 74-75*
*printing, 76*
*views, changing, 76*
Go To command, 63
opening, 73
Journal Options dialog box, 37
Junk E-Mail command (message context menu), 48
Junk E-Mail menu commands (Add to Junk Senders List), 48
Junk E-Mail tab, 49, 94
Junk Email folder, moving junk email messages to, 49
junk email messages
color coding, 94
filtering, 94
moving to Junk Email folder, 49
sorting, 48, 94

## K-L

Keep an Updated Copy of This Task on My Task List check box, 128
keyboard shortcuts, 78
keys, Alt (opening menu commands), 78

large icons, 31
links, 78. *See also* email
Click Here, 94
entering, 78
following, 78

list boxes
Stationery, 122
Type of View, 133
Use This Signature by Default, 119, 133
lists
All Attendees, 80
Change Your View, 93
Commands, 130
Favorites, 52
Inbox, 43
Print Styles, 105
Location text box, 49
Look For text box, 55

## M

mail. *See* email
Mail Format tab, 62, 119, 122, 132, 138
mail messages. *See* email
managing
files, 53
folders, 58
manual archives, 16
manual Journal entries, 74-75
Map Network Drive command (Tools menu), 54
Mark Complete button, 128
marking
email messages as read/ unread, 44, 79
flagged items as complete, 57
Maximize button, 79
maximizing windows, 79, 113
Meeting form, 81
meeting requests, copying contacts into, 29-30
meetings, 83. *See also* appointments; calendar; email
autopicking time, 82
end times, setting, 81
inviting, 81
planning, 80-82

requests, responding to, 83
responses, tracking, 82
scheduling, 79
start time, setting, 81

menu commands, opening (Alt key), 78

menus
customizing commands, 31-32
personalized, 31

message context menu command (Junk E-Mail), 48

messages. *See* email, messages

Messages tab, 55

Messages toolbar, 52

Microsoft Outlook command (Programs menu), 90

Microsoft Outlook icon, 90

Microsoft Word, 138

Microsoft Word command (New Mail Using menu), 138

Microsoft Word to Edit E-Mail Messages check box, 138

Minimize button, 83

minimizing windows, 83

modes, changing between, 4

More Buttons button, 46, 129

More Choices tab, 55

moving. *See also* copying
appointments, 13
items, 72, 84-85
junk email messages to Junk Email folder, 49

Multiple Pages button, 106

My Computer, viewing files, 53-54

My Computer button, 53, 59

My Computer files, 59

My Computer folder, 59

My Documents button, 54, 59

My Documents files, 59

My Documents folder, 54, 59

My Shortcuts, 85

My Shortcuts group button, 95

## N

Name of New View text box, 133

Name text box, 85

naming
folders, 58
personal distribution list, 101

navigating
email messages, 43
Web, 136

Net Folders, 85. *See also* email
creating, 85-86
permission status, assigning, 86
posting to, 87
publishing, 86-87
subscriber list, creating, 86
updating, 87

New All Day Event command (Actions menu), 49

New button, 45

New Call dialog box, 16

New command (File menu), 101, 137

New Distribution List command (Actions menu), 101

New Folder command
File menu, 85
Folder menu, 58

New Mail Using command (Actions menu), 138

New Mail Using menu commands (Microsoft Word), 138

New Meeting Request to Contact command (Actions menu), 82

New menu commands
Distribution List, 101
Outlook Bar Shortcut to Web Page, 137
Post in This Folder, 87

# N

**162**

New Task command (Actions menu), 125

New Task Request command (Actions menu), 128

Next Item button, 43

Note Options dialog box, 90

Notes, 88

notes
color, changing, 38, 89-90
customizing features, 38
deleting, 90
dragging, 89
editing, 89
font, changing, 38
Note folder, adding, 89
resizing, 89
sizing, 38

Notes Folder
notes, adding, 89
opening, 88

Notes icon, 88

Notes tab, 102

Number of Copies text box, 105

## O

Office Assistant, 64-65
customizing, 65
hiding, 65
settings, 65
sounds, turning on/off, 66
tip of the day, turning on/off, 66
turning off, 66

offline, working, 139

One Page button, 106

online meetings, planning, 82

Open File button, 109

Open File for Editing command (File menu), 109

opening
Contacts folder, 131
drafts, 47
file attachments, 53
files, 54

items, 71
Journal, 73
menu commands (Alt key), 78
Notes Folder, 88
Organize pane, 91
Outbox, 95
Outlook, 90-91

option buttons, Today's Tasks, 99

Options command (Tools menu), 14, 62, 79, 103, 110-112, 118-119, 132, 138

Options dialog box, 14, 79, 103, 110, 116-119, 132, 138

Organize pane, 91
closing, 92
opening, 91

Organize tool, 91

organizing
items
*categories*, 92-93
*folders*, 92
*views*, 93
messages, 93

Other Shortcut icons, 59

Other Shortcuts, 94

Other Shortcuts group button, 95

Other tab, 103, 110, 112

Outbox, 94-95. *See also* email
opening, 95
sending email messages from, 44, 95

Outbox folder, 95

Outlook
exiting, 51
opening, 90-91

Outlook Bar, 95
groups, 96
viewing/hiding, 95

Outlook Bar menu commands
Add New Group, 96
Outlook Bar Shortcut, 97
Remove Group, 96
Rename Group, 96

# 163

# INDEX

Outlook Bar Shortcut command (Outlook Bar menu), 97

Outlook Bar Shortcut to Web Page command (New menu), 137

Outlook Shortcuts group button, 95

Outlook Today page, 98
calendar days, setting, 99
customizing, 99
email messages, setting to appear, 99
setting as default, 98
tasks, setting to appear, 99
viewing, 98

Outlook.exe file, 91

## P

page setup, 100, 107

Page Setup command (File menu), 107-108

Page Setup dialog box, 107-108

Page Setup menu commands (Define Print Styles), 108

page setup options, changing (Print Preview), 106-107

pages
default, setting, 98
Outlook Today, 98-99

panes
Organize, 91-92
Preview, 42, 102-104. *See also* email
*customizing, 103-104*
*resizing, 103*
*turning on/off, 103*
Schedule, 50

Paper tab, 107-108

Paste command (Edit menu), 84, 100

pasting, 84, 100. *See also* copying

permission status (Net Folders), assigning, 86

personal distribution list, 101-102

personalized menus, 31

Phone A Contact. *See* AutoDialer

phoning contacts
AutoDialer, 16-17
speed dialing, 17-18

Plain Text command (Format menu), 62, 123

Plain Text format, 46

Plan a Meeting, 79

Plan a Meeting command (Actions menu), 80

Plan a Meeting dialog box, 80

planning meetings, 80-82

Post in This Folder command (New menu), 87

posting to Net Folders, 87

postponing reminders (snooze), 113

Preferences tab, 79, 110, 118

Preview pane, 42, 102. *See also* email
customizing, 103-104
resizing, 103
turning on/off, 103

Preview Pane command (View menu), 42, 103

Preview Pane dialog box, 103

previewing
email messages, 42
files, 109

Previous Item button, 43

Print button, 104

Print command (File menu), 104

Print dialog box, 104, 108

Print Preview, 105-107

Print Preview command (File menu), 105

Print Preview window, 105

Print Quality tab, 108

print range, specifying, 105

print styles
  default settings, 108
  editing, 108
  selecting, 105

Print Styles list, 105

printers
  changing, 104
  properties, changing, 108

printing, 104-105
  appointments, 14
  contacts, 26
  help topics, 68
  Journal entries, 76

priority
  email messages, setting, 47-48
  printer, changing, 108
  tasks, setting, 125

Priority drop-down list, 125

Programs menu commands
  (Microsoft Outlook), 90

Properties dialog box, 15, 87, 108

Publish My Free/Busy Information
  check box, 80

publishing
  free/busy times, 79-80
  Net Folders, 86-87

Push Pin button, 60

## Q-R

QuickView, 109

QuickView toolbar, 109

QuickView window, 109

read receipts, 48

reading email messages, 43

recurring appointments, 11. *See
  also* appointments

recurring events, setting, 50

Redo command (Edit menu), 110

redoing actions, 109

Refresh Current Page button, 136

Reminder, 110

Reminder check box, 111, 126

Reminder Options dialog
  box, 111-112

Reminder prompt box, 113

reminders. *See also* appointments,
  Calendar, contacts, tasks
  alarm, changing sound, 112
  assigning, 12
    *appointments, 111*
    *contacts, 111-112*
    *tasks, 111*
  default settings, changing, 110
  dismissing, 112
  postponing (snooze), 113
  setting, 110

Remove Group command
  (Outlook Bar menu), 96

removing
  buttons (toolbars), 129
  entries (personal distribution
    list), 102
  flags, 57

Rename Group command
  (Outlook Bar menu), 96

renaming
  folders, 59
  groups (Outlook Bar), 96
  rules, 115
  shortcuts, 97
  views, 135

replying to email messages, 43-44

Request a Read Receipt for This
  Message check box, 48

requests (tasks), sending, 128

resetting default settings
  (toolbars), 130

resizing
  notes, 89
  Preview pane, 103

responding to meeting requests, 83

responses (meetings), tracking, 82

Restore button, 113

restoring size (windows), 113

Rich Text command
Format menu, 62
View menu, 46

Rich Text format, 46

rules, 113
deleting, 115
editing, 115
exporting, 116
importing, 116
organizing messages with, 93
renaming, 115
running, 115
setting, 114
turning on/off, 114

Rules Wizard, 113

Rules Wizard command (Tools menu), 114

Rules Wizard dialog box, 114

running rules, 115

## S

Save As command (File menu), 117

Save As dialog box, 117

Save As Web Page command (File menu), 137

Save Changes button, 98

Save Copies of Messages in Sent Items Folder check box, 118

Save Exported Rules As dialog box, 116

saving, 117
Calendar as Web page, 137
contacts as vCards, 131
file attachments, 53, 117
items, 117
sent email messages, 118
unfinished email messages, 118
vCards, 132

Schedule. *See* Calendar

Schedule pane, 50

scheduling
appointments, 10-11
events, 49-50
meetings, 79

Search the Web button, 137

searching. *See* finding

Select Attendees and Resources dialog box, 81

Select Folder dialog box, 99

Select Group Members dialog box, 7

Select Members dialog box, 101

selecting
items, 71
print styles, 105
Web pages (Favorites menu), 135

selecting items, 28

Send Me a Status Report When This Task Is Complete check box, 128

Send Message to Contact button, 47

Send/Receive command (Tools menu), 41

Send Web Page by E-mail command (Actions menu), 137

sending
email messages, 44, 95
requests (tasks), 128
vCards in email messages, 132
Web pages in email, 137

sensitivity (email messages), setting, 47-48

sent email messages, saving, 118

Sent Items folder, 118

services, viewing, 3

Services command (Tools menu), 3

Services dialog box, 3

setting
appointments, 10-11
calendar days (Outlook Today page), 99

default format (email
   messages), 62
default pages (Outlook
   Today), 98
email messages to appear
   (Outlook Today page), 99
end times
   *events, 49*
   *meetings, 81*
priority
   *email messages, 47-48*
   *tasks, 125*
recurring events, 50
reminders, 110
rules, 114
sensitivity (email
   messages), 47-48
start times
   *events, 49*
   *meetings, 81*
status (tasks), 125, 128
Task Reminder
   options, 110-111
tasks to appear (Outlook Today
   page), 99
settings
   default (print styles), 108
   email messages, 48
Settings command (Start
   menu), 91
Settings menu commands (Taskbar
   & Start), 91
Share command (File menu), 86
Share menu commands (This
   Folder), 86
Sharing tab, 87
shortcuts
   Favorites, 59
   groups, 97
   icons, changing size, 97
   keyboard, 78
   renaming, 97
   viewing, 95
   Web pages, adding to Outlook
      bar, 137

show time as setting
   (appointments), 12
Signature command (Insert
   menu), 119
Signature Picker dialog
   box, 119, 133
signatures, 35, 119
   creating, 119
   deleting, 121
   editing, 120
   inserting, 119-120
   vCards, attaching, 132-133
sizing
   Calendar panes, 20
   notes, 38
snooze (reminders), 113
sorting
   email messages, 70
   junk email messages, 48, 94
specifying print range, 105
speed dialing, 17-18
Spell Check, 121-122
spelling, checking, 121-122
Spelling command (Tools
   menu), 121
Spelling dialog box, 122
Standard and Formatting Toolbars
   Share One Row check box, 47
Standard toolbar, 47, 129, 135
Start menu commands
   (Settings), 91
Start button, 137
Start Menu Programs tab, 91
start times, setting
   events, 49
   meetings, 81
Startup folder, 38, 91
stationery, 122-123. *See also* email
   customizing, 123
   turning on/off, 123-124
Stationery list box, 122
Stationery Picker dialog box, 122

status (tasks), setting, 125, 128

Status drop-down list, 125, 128

Stop Current Jump button, 136

Subject text box, 45, 49, 125

# T

tabs
  Advanced, 56
  Attendee Availability, 82
  Commands, 130
  Details, 126
  Device Options, 108
  Fonts, 108
  Format, 106
  Header/Footer, 107
  Junk E-Mail, 49, 94
  Mail Format, 62, 119, 122,
    132, 138
  Messages, 55
  More Choices, 55
  Notes, 102
  Other, 103, 110-112
  Paper, 107-108
  Preferences, 79, 110, 118
  Print Quality, 108
  Sharing, 87
  Start Menu Programs, 91
  Task, 125
  Toolbars, 129
  Using Categories, 92
  Using Colors, 93
  Using Folders, 92-93
  Using Views, 93

Task button, 126-127

Task List, 126-127

Task Reminder options,
  setting, 110-111

Task tab, 125

Taskbar & Start menu command
  (Settings menu), 91

Taskbar Properties dialog box, 91

TaskPad, adding tasks from, 127

tasks, 124. *See also* reminders
  adding, 126-127
  copying into appointments, 30
  customizing features, 36
  deleting, 127
  editing, 127
  Outlook Today page, setting to
    appear, 99
  priority, setting, 125
  reminders, assigning to, 111
  requests, sending, 128
  status, setting, 125, 128

Tasks button, 125

Tasks folder, 124

text (forms), copying, 29

text boxes
  Bcc, 46
  Calendar Title, 137
  Cc, 45
  File Name, 52, 117, 138
  Location, 49
  Look For, 55
  Name, 85
  Name of New View, 133
  Number of Copies, 105
  Subject, 45, 49, 125

text files (TXT), 117

This Folder command (Share
  menu), 86

This Is an Online Meeting Using
  check box, 82

tip of the day, turning on/off, 66

Today's Tasks option button, 99

toolbars, 129
  buttons, removing, 129
  customizing, 32-33, 129-130
  default settings, resetting, 130
  displaying, 129
  Event, 50
  Formatting, 46-47
  hiding, 129
  Message, 52
  QuickView, 109
  Standard, 47, 129, 135
  Web, 135

Toolbars command (View menu), 129,135

Toolbars menu commands (Web), 135

Toolbars tab, 129

tools
Find, 54
Organize, 91

Tools menu commands
Accounts, 1
Customize, 31, 47, 129
Forms, 61
Map Network Drive, 54
Options, 14, 62, 79, 103, 110-112, 118-119, 132, 138
Rules Wizard, 114
Send/Receive, 41
Services, 3
Spelling, 121

Tracking Options settings, 48

tracking responses (meetings), 82

turning on/off
Preview pane, 103
rules, 114
stationery, 123-124

TXT (text files), 117

Type of View list box, 133

## U-V

Undo command (Edit menu), 130

undoing actions, 130

unfinished email messages, saving, 118

Uniform Resource Locators (URLs), 135-136

updating
Net Folders, 87
personal distribution list, 101

URLs (Uniform Resource Locators), 135-136

Use Background Graphic check box, 137

Use This Signature by Default list box, 119, 133

Using Categories tab, 92

Using Color tabs, 93

Using Folders tab, 92-93

Using Views tab, 93

vCard attachments, viewing, 132

vCards (virtual business cards), 131. See also contacts; email
attaching (signatures), 132-133
importing, 131
saving, 132
saving contacts as, 131
sending in email messages, 132

View menu commands
AutoPreview, 42
Bcc, 46
Current View, 133-134
Folder List, 59-60
Go To, 63
HTML, 46
Preview Pane, 42, 103
Rich Text, 46
Toolbars, 129, 135

View Settings dialog box, 134

View Summary dialog box, 134

viewing
attachments (QuickView), 109
buttons, 129
files, 53-54, 59
Folder List, 60
folders, 59
Outlook Bar, 95
pages (Outlook Today), 98
shortcuts, 95
vCard attachments, 132

views, 133
by Category, 22
Calendar, changing, 19-20
changing, 133
contacts, changing, 25
custom, deleting, 135

customizing, 133-134
Inbox, changing, 70
Journal entries, 76
Notes, changing, 88
organizing items by, 93
renaming, 135

virtual business cards. *See* vCards

## W-Z

Web, navigating, 136

Web addresses, 135

Web command (Toolbars menu), 135

Web pages, 51, 78, 135. *See also* links
saving Calendar as, 137
selecting (Favorites menu), 135
sending in email, 137
shortcuts, adding to Outlook bar, 137

Web toolbar, 135

What's This? (help), 69

When Starting, Go Directly to Outlook Today check box, 98

windows
Help, navigating, 67
maximizing, 79
minimizing, 83
Print Preview, 105
QuickView, 109
restoring size, 113

wizards
Import and Export, 8
Rules, 113

Word, 138

Work Offline command (File menu), 139

working offline, 139

writing email messages, 45

Yearly Events/Occurrences. *See* events

## Get FREE books and more...when you register this book online for our Personal Bookshelf Program

*http://register.quecorp.com/*

Register online and you can sign up for our *FREE Personal Bookshelf Program...* unlimited access to the electronic version of more than 200 complete computer books—immediately! That means you'll have 100,000 pages of valuable information onscreen, at your fingertips!

Plus, you can access product support, including complimentary downloads, technical support files, book-focused links, companion Web sites, author sites, and more!

And you'll be automatically registered to receive a *FREE subscription to our weekly email newsletter* to help you stay current with news, announcements, sample book chapters, and special events including sweepstakes, contests, and various product giveaways!

We value your comments! Best of all, the entire registration process takes only a few minutes to complete, so go online and get the greatest value going—absolutely FREE!

## Don't Miss Out on This Great Opportunity!

QUE® is a brand of Macmillan Computer Publishing USA.

For more information, please visit *www.mcp.com*

Copyright ©1999 Macmillan Computer Publishing USA